REAL CHANGE

BECOMING MORE LIKE JESUS
IN EVERYDAY LIFE

Andrew Nicholls and Helen Thorne

David Powlison, Editor

New
Growth
Press

WWW.NEWGROWTHPRESS.COM

New Growth Press, Greensboro, NC 27401

Cover Design: Jon Bradley, ninefootone creative;
                Tom Temple, Tandem Creative
Interior Typesetting and eBook: Lisa Parnell, lparnell.com

ISBN: 978-1-948130-03-5 (Print US)
ISBN: 978-1-948130-89-9 (Print UK)
ISBN: 978-1-948130-04-2 (eBook)

Printed in the United States of America

25 24 23 22 21 20 19 18   1 2 3 4 5

CONTENTS

INTRODUCTION

Welcome to *Real Change*! In this six-session course, you will learn more about how God changes us. It is an opportunity for you to grow in faith, in love, and in hope. It is an opportunity for you to become more like Jesus. He expressed the honest faith of the Psalms. He lived the practical wisdom of the Proverbs. He embodied the self-giving love that expresses the purposes of God's heart.

All of us have hearts that go astray; all of us face troubles that weigh on us. But Christ meets us where we are, in the places where we struggle. God promises to work patiently with us in the midst of our wayward-ness and our woes. Faith meets God in the very place of honest struggle with sin and affliction. His mercy and grace change us in ways that are truly beautiful and joyous. You can trust the words of Philippians 1:6: "I am sure of this, that he who began a good work in you will bring it to completion at the day of Jesus Christ" (ESV).

Each week the Bible study, reflection, and discussion in *Real Change* will help you understand how God works with us. You will reflect on your own heart. You will reflect on life's hardships. You will reflect on God's mercies. And you will come to better understand how your Savior meets you in your particular life situation.

If you are doing this study in a group, your leader(s) will guide your time together. Each week you will be encouraged to share some of what you are learning with one or two others in the group. If you are doing this study on your own, we encourage you to tell someone else what God is showing you. Real change is not a self-improvement project that we do entirely on our own! We grow nearer to God both by his direct working and by the encouragement and prayers of other people.

Throughout the course you will be asked to undertake a "change project." This involves choosing one aspect of your life where you would like to see growth. From week to week, you will begin to address it by bringing it under the mercies of Jesus Christ. Please don't expect to be perfect by the end of six weeks! (That won't happen until Jesus returns or calls us home.) But we hope you will begin to move toward God in your area of struggle and that you will have the privilege of experiencing God's help.

During each session, there are times set aside to discuss and apply what you are learning. We recommend these discussion times be done with one other person. Since you will be looking at the teaching of the Bible and discussing aspects of your change project, continuity will be important. So we recommend you keep the same discussion partner throughout the course. A discussion group of just two people will work much better than larger groupings of three or more. Of course, if your discussion partner is not able to attend one week, you will have to join with another group for that session.

Between each of the six sessions you will have some homework to do—some reading, reflecting, and journaling (writing down a few of your thoughts). Please set aside time for this. To be self-reflective is an important part of the process of change. It helps us take to heart what God is saying. And please be praying for yourself, your leader(s), and the other members of the group as you go through this material. We are all utterly reliant on the Lord.

CHANGE

AIM

To help you reflect on the need for change and the certainty of change. To provide a brief overview of the process of change.

READ

LIVES IN NEED OF CHANGE

You're driving your car on your way into the city. It's a friend's birthday and a group is going to meet up for dinner and a show. You have been looking forward to the celebration all day. You haven't seen this particular friend for years, and you've heard she has recently become a Christian. You're eager to catch up with all that has been going on.

You were a little late starting your journey. Just before leaving the house, you got a phone call from your mother, which was going to be "just a quick one." You answered out of a desire to be kind to her. But it wasn't so quick. As a result, you left home behind schedule and already in a rush.

However, the drive starts well, and it seems the delay will be of little consequence. Until, that is, you look at your fuel gauge—you're running on fumes. There's nothing else for it; you will have to stop. It's going to take you further out of your way, but you need the fuel. As you pay, you look at your watch a little anxiously. There had been some slack in your travel timetable, but that was before your detour. Now things are getting tight. You promised your friends you would be there ten minutes before the birthday girl arrived so you could all surprise her. If you can't make up the time, you won't be there before her. You remember with a flutter of anxiety that you have the theater tickets, so no one can get in without you. But you aren't that late, so you are not too worried. You try to call your friends to give a heads up about not being there for the surprise, but none of them answers the phone.

You restart your journey, hopeful you might just make it in time. But there's been an accident ahead. The traffic is stopped, then barely crawls. You could walk more quickly! When you finally get moving, a glance at the time confirms that this evening's performance will begin in approximately twenty-five minutes. There's no hope of joining your friends ahead of time. But you might just make it for the beginning of the show.

After another ten minutes, you reach your destination and begin looking for a parking space. You spot one on the corner, but another car beats you to it. After going around a couple more blocks, you finally find a spot. You have seven minutes to make the show. The theater is eight minutes away if you walk *very* briskly.

REFLECT

How are you feeling right now? What is going through your mind? You may be experiencing a range of emotions! Take a moment to think through why you are experiencing those particular emotions. If you are anxious, what exactly are you anxious about? If you are frustrated, who are you angry at? If you are despairing, what hopes have been dashed? Since you are letting others down by being late, how do you imagine they feel, and how does that affect you right now?

Share your thoughts with the group.

THE STORY IS NOT OVER, SO READ ON.

As you are running along, you bump into a good friend from church. She is standing outside a coffee shop in tears. You can immediately guess why. The two of you had talked last Sunday about the new man in her life who had just invited her on a first date. This must be it! She had been excited about the possibility of a relationship ahead, but she was delayed at work and then got stuck in a traffic jam even worse than yours. She is now more than an hour late for their coffee date. She had forgotten to charge her phone, so she can't even access his phone number. He has long since given up waiting for her. Her mascara, of which there is plenty, is clearly not waterproof. She looks a mess, but might not be aware of it. She latches on to you with a look of panic and anger, saying, "Why did this have to happen now? Why would God do that?"

REFLECT

You are going in the same direction, so you can kind of talk as you hurry along. Given how your day is going, what are you thinking in your head? What would you say out loud?

Once you have honestly reflected on how you think you would respond, reflect on whether there are other ways you could respond that could be more helpful. What truth about God would you want your friend to remember at a time like this? What truth about God have you both forgotten? How might that truth also touch you?

This is ordinary life: a life with many stresses, choices, and opportunities. We all have our natural way of doing things—the ways we instinctively respond to annoyance and trouble. There are things we instinctively want (like getting our own way!). There are things that make us feel stressed and anxious. We all react in ways that are not constructive. The Bible calls these desires, fears, and reactions your "old self." But as Christians, something else is also going on with us. We have Christ. He is the gift that is beyond words (2 Corinthians 9:15). To belong to him, to be one with him, to know him, and to grow in relationship with him—this is your "new self" (Ephesians 4:22–24).

This course aims to help you turn away from your old self with all its self-centered desires and to put on your new self with all its Christ-centered purposes. We are going to think together about *how* we change to become more like Christ. It's a process, so don't expect change to happen overnight. But do expect to grow in understanding. And do expect to begin changing. All of us who belong to Jesus are being changed to become like him.

LIVES IN A CONTEXT OF CHANGE

If you could change anything you wanted about yourself, what would it be?

GOD IS CHANGING EACH OF US

READ: 2 CORINTHIANS 3:18

Discuss the following questions.

1. Who is working to transform us? How certain is our transformation?

2. What are we being changed into? What excites you about this?

God is not reluctant to change his children. We might be like run-down houses that need lots of renovation, but God never thinks, "What a wreck! I can't be bothered with them." He knows what we will one day become. He knows we will be beautiful when he completes his work in us, and he loves to change us little by little to become more like Jesus.

GOD IS CHANGING US THROUGH OUR RELATIONSHIP WITH JESUS

The way we view Jesus will affect our view of how he is going to change us.

» How do you think of your relationship with Jesus? (Check all that apply.)

☐ He's the boss. I'm the employee.

☐ He has befriended me. I am his friend.

☐ He is the teacher. I am learning from him.

☐ He is the husband. I am his bride.

☐ He is my shepherd. I am a sheep.

☐ Something different?

God, in his Word, gives us all of these ways of understanding our relationship with Christ—and more—so we can understand his love, care, concern, and tenderness toward us. They are all brought together under one central concept: we are united to Christ. Paul, in Ephesians 1, calls this being "in Christ."

READ: EPHESIANS 1:1–14

Discuss the following questions.

3. How is our relationship with Christ repeatedly described?

4. What difference does it make if we are united to Christ? Why does it matter how we think about our relationship with Jesus?

5. What is the outcome of this unity for us (vv. 4, 14)? And for God (vv. 3, 6, 12, 14)?

Being united with Christ changes everything. In Christ we have all the blessings he has! When we are "in Christ," we are on a new path toward a wonderful destination—holy, blameless, and fully redeemed. God will be praised forever for his glorious grace in choosing us and transforming us to live under Christ's rule. All this is *Real Change*—total transformation—and it all happens only through being "in Christ." For the next six weeks, we will be unpacking the details of what it means to be in Christ and how being united with Christ brings change to our desires, thoughts, words, and actions. It won't be complete until we see him face to face, but we are now in the process of changing to be like him (1 John 3:1–3).

GOD IS CHANGING US THROUGH OUR RELATIONSHIPS WITH OTHER CHRISTIANS

READ: EPHESIANS 4:11–16
Discuss the following question.

6. How do our relationships with one another promote change?

We read the apostles and prophets. We listen to pastors and teachers and perhaps evangelists. These people are Jesus's gifts to us to help us grow. Once we have listened to these gifted people, we need to serve and speak to one another, passing on what we have heard and connecting it lovingly with the circumstances of one another's lives. When we speak and listen to one another, we help one another mature under Christ's rule. Just as a body is made up of many different parts that all depend on one another to keep the body functioning, Jesus has made it so that we desperately need one another to stay and grow in Christ's body, the church.

Churches are *very exciting places*! Here God's people are being used by him to help one another grow up into Christ.

A MODEL FOR UNDERSTANDING CHANGE FROM JEREMIAH 17:5-8

READ: JEREMIAH 17:5-8

This is what the LORD says:
"Cursed is the one who trusts in man,
    who draws strength from mere flesh
    and whose heart turns away from the LORD.
6 That person will be like a bush in the wastelands;
    they will not see prosperity when it comes.
They will dwell in the parched places of the desert,
    in a salt land where no one lives.
7 "But blessed is the one who trusts in the LORD,
    whose confidence is in him.
8 They will be like a tree planted by the water
    that sends out its roots by the stream.
It does not fear when heat comes;
    its leaves are always green.
It has no worries in a year of drought
    and never fails to bear fruit."

Jeremiah uses a vivid metaphor to help us understand the process of change.[1] He gives us a picture of two trees. One is a stunted bush in the desert and the other is flourishing by the water. When drought comes (as it always does in that part of the world), one tree withers while the other tree stays green. Its roots are connected to the stream of water. Jeremiah's point is that the person who trusts in God is like a tree that stays green in drought. Even when hard times come (as they always do), the person who is rooted in the life-giving stream of God's love will continue to bear the fruit of love for God and others. This metaphor is the starting point for a model of change that takes into account "the heat" in our lives (our hard times, temptations, etc.), but also unpacks why we respond the way we do and how being in Christ brings transformation.

---

1. This model of change was developed by David Powlison for the CCEF course, *Dynamics of Biblical Change.*

» The **Heat**. These are the situations we all face (like being late for a birthday celebration) that put us under pressure. They can literally make us hot! Of course, this also refers to much more serious difficulties, such as illness, death, financial struggles, broken relationships, parenting problems, emotional struggles, etc. But good things can also put us under pressure. Getting a raise at work, moving to a nice house, or getting married can also bring challenges in our relationship with God.

» **Root/Heart**. This is the decision-making center of who we are (the Bible sometimes calls it the soul, mind, heart, or will). It is the place where we decide how we are going to respond to what is going on around us and to God. When we are rooted in our old self and old way of doing things, our desires, thoughts, and actions will be self-focused and without love for God and others—what the Bible calls "sin."

» **Thorns**. These are the God-dishonoring, self-focused ways we respond to the heat of life (like being angry with people who take "our" parking spot). These things stem from the self-centered desires of our hearts. The Bible, and our diagram, also call this "bad fruit."

» **Reap** (negative consequences). This is how we respond to the heat in our lives, which also affects those around us. Our decision to respond in a self-focused way negatively affects our relationships and the situation we are in.

» **Lifegiving Spirit**. This is the stream of living water, the Holy Spirit, who flows from Christ to us. The Spirit meets us in our sinfulness, helps us to repent at the foot of the cross, emboldens our faith, and then brings about change in our hearts and lives.

» **Cross**. This represents all the promises of God's mercy, culminating in Jesus's death and resurrection. Through the cross of Christ, our "bad root" is transformed. We are forgiven. We are given a new life. We are connected to streams of living water—the Spirit of Christ. It's in going to Jesus and asking for forgiveness for our self-centered desires, thoughts, and actions that transformation begins and continues. Change happens as the Spirit brings us to the God of mercies.

» **Good root.** The "Repentance and Faith" arrow shows how the process of change is a living dynamic that relates us to Christ through his Spirit through repentance and in faith. This is not a "one and done" process at the beginning of the Christian life or in response to a major crisis. We need to go to Jesus every day for forgiveness, hope, and help. As we learn to go to Jesus every day, our roots go down deep into him, the life-giving stream. He gives us his life (the good root). In Christ, our desires, thoughts, and actions gradually change to be like him.

» **Good fruit.** These are the God-honoring ways we can respond to the heat of life: behaviors, thoughts, and actions that stem from the godly desires of our hearts (like loving distressed friends enough to listen to them and share Jesus with them even when we are running late). Good fruit is expressed in love for God and others. The "Love" arrow from the fruit tree toward the heat stands for the living dynamic of how being in Christ moves us into our world constructively with a growing love for God and people.

» **Reap** (positive consequences). When we respond to our heat in Christ, this results in positive consequences that bless us, those around us, and the situation we are in. God's promise is we will be blessed and also be a blessing. That doesn't mean the heat will go away, but it does mean God will help us live fruitful lives of love toward him and others despite the hard circumstances we encounter.

Below is the Three Trees diagram that puts all of these different elements together. Through the next six weeks, we will be learning how this diagram applies to our choices and behavior. Hopefully this diagram will give you useful categories for understanding your heart and your actions and also help you to understand the work of Christ through his Spirit in you and for you.

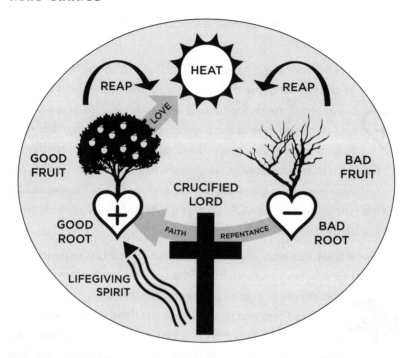

HOMEWORK

During this course you have an opportunity to undertake a change project. This week, ask God to help you live with a greater awareness of what is going on around you. (See if you can tune in to your "heat.") As you go through the week, try to notice times when you are struggling. Where are the hard spots in your life? What are you finding difficult? Your struggles can come in many forms: a challenging relationship, physical health, work problems, disappointments, injustice, your circumstances, unwelcome news, or being treated badly. Remember too that having things easy is also a challenge. Are there parts of your life that are so easy or successful that God seems unnecessary or irrelevant? What in your situation makes it easy to leave God to one side? Considering these things will help you decide what particular area of your life your change project should address.

It will help you to write down your thoughts. Even if they feel jumbled and uncertain, writing down specific areas of "heat" in your life will give you clarity on what your change project should be.

HEAT

AIMS

To help you reflect on the ways in which your circumstances affect your heart, and to enable you to begin your journey of change.

RECAP

» God is transforming us into the image of his Son.

» God is transforming and changing all of us in our relationships with Christ and one another.

Sometimes it can seem appealing to look for some shortcut to change. We can tell ourselves that if we just exercise more self-control, or try harder, or find an accountability partner, we'll be fine. But changing to be more like Jesus isn't about tweaking our behavior, it's about having our hearts transformed and our lives reorientated in relationship with God. There are no shortcuts to real change.

HEAT - THORNS - CROSS - FRUIT

READ: JEREMIAH 17:5-14

All of us face heat—the pressures of life that come at us from all directions (v. 8).

In the midst of those circumstances, all of us can be like the man who trusts in "flesh." That simply means trusting in what you can accomplish without depending on God. That person, says Jeremiah, will be like a bush dwelling in the parched places of the desert. When we live like that, responding without the Lord's influence, we bear thorns (vv. 5–6).

In the middle of those same circumstances, all of us who are in Christ can be like the man who trusts in the LORD. To live by faith is to be like a tree planted by the water that sends out its roots by the stream. When we live in dependent relationship with Christ, we bear good fruit (vv. 7–8).

To turn from bearing thorns and to grow in bearing fruit, we need to acknowledge our heart is wayward (v. 9). The Lord knows this already, because he can see our deepest motivations and desires (v. 10). Without God, we desire to go our own way, depending only on ourselves for help. God calls us to turn to him (and away from self-dependence) in our circumstances for hope (v. 13) and transformation (v. 14).

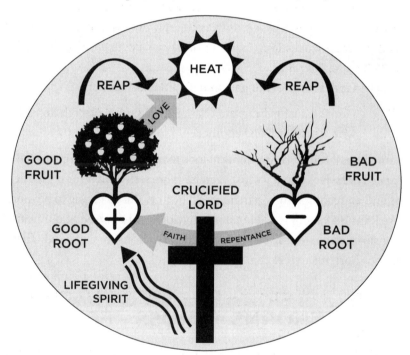

REFLECT

What are some of the pressures (the heat) in your life right now?

Relationship with my parents - their views on how my children behave Dad's stubborness mum's weakness

What is the specific heat you noticed in your life last week when you did your homework? In what ways do you tend to respond to that heat?

Anxiety → depression

Defensiveness

Share what you have observed with your discussion partner. Take three minutes to share the heat of your situation. What is happening that is hard or challenging? What are other people doing that feels difficult? What things or circumstances around you make it difficult to live well (they can be either poverty or riches)?

DISCUSS

Next, allow two minutes for your discussion partner to ask you questions. Then switch so your discussion partner can share about his or her heat and you can ask questions. In asking questions, your goal is not to pry, but to understand as much as you can about another's situation. What pressures or distractions is the person facing? What challenge is the person identifying? What factors make it challenging? In what circumstances is it felt most acutely? Why then?

At the end, write a summary sentence about your discussion partner's struggles here:

GOD UNDERSTANDS MY SITUATION

READ: PSALM 22:1-21

1. What heat is the psalmist experiencing in these verses? What is Jesus experiencing when he fulfills the words of this psalm, which he quotes on the cross (Mark 15:34)?

Total exposure

God turning his back

Our God is truly wonderful! When he came as Immanuel, God with us, he did not live in wealth and success. He experienced the deepest possible human struggles. He is able to understand our situations. He meets us in them and rescues us from them.

Even more wonderful, until the day comes when he rescues us from all that is hard and wrong, God uses our struggles to make us more like Christ and to deepen our fellowship with him.

READ: 1 PETER 1:3-9

2. The church to whom Peter was writing was facing "all kinds of trials." Writing about these difficulties, Peter tells them their trials are under God's control, bringing them something they need even more than an end to their problems. What is that?

Salvation of their souls

3. What response can we make in trials when we trust what God is doing?

Praise, glory + honour to God.
Ask to be changed to be more like Jesus.

We often want God to take away our trials, and sometimes he does. But always he uses our trials and troubles to change us in immeasurably precious and important ways, bringing us deep joy even in the midst of the hardest times.

4. What image does Peter use for what God is forming in us? How does this give you hope?

Refining fire - purifying

GOD ENABLES ME TO GROW IN RESPONSE TO MY SITUATION

READ: NUMBERS 11:4–15

5. How are the Israelites reacting to the trials they are experiencing?

READ: DEUTERONOMY 8:2–3

6. Why were these things happening to them?

The Israelites forgot the hardships of Egypt and thought God had brought them into the desert to die. They grumbled repeatedly and thought they were better off as slaves. However, God wanted what was best for them. He was humbling them, teaching them dependence, and showing them there is more to life than food.

READ: 1 CORINTHIANS 10:1–11

7. In light of this passage, what else can we learn about why these things were happening to them?

The Israelites' experiences are also designed to teach us, warning us to learn from their experience. Our troubles and temptations need not take us away from God, because he always gives us what we need to respond in a way that pleases him. He is always enabling us to grow amid the difficulties of our situation. While we don't always respond well, he is always at work through his Spirit, convicting us and turning our hearts back to him for the help we need.

DISCUSS

Read your summary sentence of your discussion partner's personal struggles and ask if you have understood the situation accurately.

With the above passages in mind, reframe your summary of your discussion partner's situation so it includes some beautiful truths about God and his good purposes. For example, if your partner's summary was "Jane has been struggling with a baby who doesn't sleep and a toddler who doesn't listen. She has been worn down over the last four weeks and is at her wit's end," your reframing could be, "God has been leading Jane through some very hard times with her children. Her normal sources of refreshment have been taken away, and she can't find her usual energy to get through her day. She has been tempted to despair, but God understands the hardship. He loves Jane deeply, and he is at work in this situation to make her grow like Christ. She can't feel any of this, but it's still true!" Or, if your summary was "Bob has been struggling with a huge workload and a very unsympathetic boss who regularly expects the impossible," your reframing could be "God has allowed the burden of Bob's work to grow a great deal recently. It's hard for Bob to love the job like he used to, but God's love for him has not changed, and he has a plan to bless Bob as he leads him through this time."

The tough times you are facing aren't cause for hopelessness but cause for hope that you can and will become more like Jesus.

HOMEWORK

Next week we will be thinking about thorns: our ungodly reactions to heat.

Think about how you respond to the situations in which you are struggling. What would people see in you that tells them things are going wrong? Over the next few days, each time you notice yourself responding badly to your heat, ask yourself some of these questions:

» What are you saying to those around you?

» With what exact words and tone of voice?

» What are you doing?

» Where are you looking (toward God or toward other people or priorities)?

» What are you wondering about doing?

» What are you thinking?

» What are you feeling?

» What words are forming but not said?

» What alternative scenarios are you playing out?

» What is happening in the moment, and what is happening afterward if you return to it in your memory?

» What thoughts are you holding on to, and nursing?

» Are there good things you are not doing?

» What is being *reaped* as you respond like this? What is the result of your "thornlike" response?

3 THORNS

AIM

To help you reflect on the ways in which the desires of your heart drive your responses to the heat of life.

RECAP

» God is changing us into the image of his Son.

» God is changing us in and through our situations.

HEAT – THORNS – CROSS – FRUIT

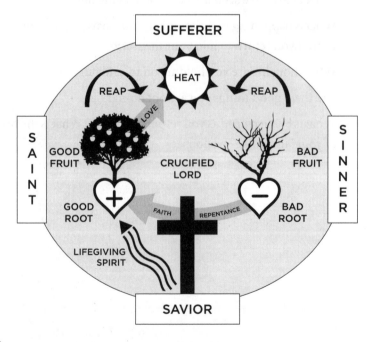

All Christians are simultaneously saint, sufferer, and sinner. As saints, we are God's children and are already being transformed by the Spirit who is at work in us. Much of this happens as we suffer, experiencing all kinds of heat that make our lives difficult. At the same time, we are also rebels who dishonor the Lord in thought, word, and deed, in sins of commission and omission. As we work through this model, this session focuses on the sin remaining in our hearts. But it's not all bad news, because God has already been lovingly at work in us, keeping his promises faithfully.

I PRODUCE THORNS

READ: COLOSSIANS 3:5-11

REFLECT

Make a note of the sinful responses to life's challenges that are listed in this passage. Underline those that are particular issues for you, and try to think of a specific situation in your life in which these responses can arise. Remember that the sins listed here can be expressed in many ways. For example, slander can include gossip, idolatry can include longing for control or some kind of ideal relationship, and greed encompasses wanting more power, influence, and/or money.

DISCUSS

Share the issues you have been thinking and praying about this week. Talk about what you have been doing, what you said, what you felt, how you responded. What were the thorns you noticed?

READ: COLOSSIANS 3:9-17

Paul sets out a process for change. He instructs us to "put off" our old way of life and "put on" Christian living as our minds are transformed. All too often, however, we don't try to "put off" our thorny behavior. There are at least seven big ways we can respond to the heat in ungodly (thorny, or "bad fruit") ways. And when we don't "put off" our thorny responses, we create more thorns. It can seem like a never-ending cycle. But don't despair. The gospel of Jesus Christ brings hope.

1. **Worry**. You fret. You go over and over the circumstances. You try to think through every possibility and come up with your own way of dealing with the problem. You are consumed with the problem and can't shut your mind off.

2. **Escapism**. You try to anesthetize yourself so you don't have to feel the heat or acknowledge how you have responded out of your old ways of doing things. This can include drug and alcohol abuse, overworking, overeating, being online, and really almost anything!

3. **Denial**. You try to ignore the problem and pretend you are okay. You hope that if others believe you are fine, that will somehow make it true.

4. **Anger and blame**. You get angry at others and blame people, circumstances, and even God. You lash out at those you feel are responsible for your bad response. "If only they hadn't done _____, then I never would have reacted the way I did."

5. **Self-pity**. You feel sorry for yourself. You want others to feel sorry for you too (this is directly related to blaming circumstances, God, and people).

6. **Fear**. You shrink back in fear. You spin out worst-case scenarios about the future. You believe your life is ruined.

7. **Despair**. All of the above can lead you to despair. You don't think you can ever change. You don't believe God is with you or will help you. Life becomes dark and hopeless.

DISCUSS

Pick two of these areas and discuss some possible consequences of these responses. If we respond (sow) like this, what might the consequences (the reaping) be for us and others? How do these responses change my situation for the worse?

Think about the issue you have been working on in your homework. Do you see yourself falling into any of the above responses? If so, discuss this with your discussion partner. Talk also about the reaping/consequences you have noticed in your own situation. How do your thorny responses change the "heat" for you and for others?

MY THORNS COME FROM MY HEART

READ: MARK 7:20–23 AND LUKE 6:43–45

DISCUSS

1. Why is there a mess in our lives?

Often we think of ourselves as basically good and believe we only react badly because of what has happened to us. If we think we're generally fine, then it can be hard to understand why we behave as we do and why it's so hard to change how we act. The Bible is clear, though, that we are not basically good. There is a serious problem with our hearts. When we see our hearts as Jesus sees them, then it's not a surprise that "thorns" spring from our hearts.

READ: JAMES 4:1–3

DISCUSS

2. What common human problem is James describing?

3. Where do these problems start from?

Arguing is a heart issue, arising from a battle raging within. When we fight back, it is because we are not getting what we want, and we are trying to make sure this changes. We try to push other people out of the way so our desires can be met.

Our hearts don't reveal themselves all at once. We might begin by expressing a preference that seems entirely reasonable. But if that preference is tied to something deep within, we won't let it go, and it grows into something we desire even more strongly. When desire grows into something we believe we really need, we feel entitled to it and become resentful of whoever keeps it from us (a spouse, a stranger driving the car in front of us, or God). Instead of having a preference for something, we end up demanding that it be supplied immediately. This doesn't mean what we might want is a bad thing in and of itself. Often it can be a good thing, such as respect, love, peace, and quiet. But once a preference becomes a desire we "need" and feel entitled to, we demand that we receive it. Then the fighting begins with those who see only their own "need."

Here is what the process looks like:

PREFERENCE → DESIRE → NEED → ENTITLEMENT → DEMAND

It's not pretty, but this really is what we are like. And it's here, in our hearts, that God must change us.

DISCUSS

With your discussion partner, share whatever thoughts you have about the particular preferences and desires motivating you. Can you see how they underlie your "thorny" responses? To help your discussion, turn to the long and varied list of diagnostic questions at the end of this session. Pick one or two that will help you unearth something important about your motivations and desires. Then tell your discussion partner so he or she can ask you the questions. Pray for each other too.

Now we are ready to ask: How can my heart and reactions be changed?

HOMEWORK

1. In preparation for next week, try to spend a few minutes bringing the heart issues you have been talking about to God. This is not simply saying, "Dear Lord, I have done this wrong again." It is saying, "Dear Father, I am the kind of person who does things like this. My heart is me, and I have been desiring/longing/blaming/running after/ hoping in _____." Spend some time looking at the story of the lost son in Luke 15:11–32. What can you see of his heart issues? Meditate on how the father responds to the repentant son. How does God respond to all those who come back to him convinced of their attitude problems? Keep talking to God about what you are finding.

2. Next sum up—in writing—what you are discovering about the specific issue you are working on. Briefly, describe the heat you are facing, the thorns you are displaying, and the desires hiding in your heart, as well as a summary of the ways in which God responds to you when you come to him in repentance. Writing this out will help to clarify your thoughts and engage you more fully with the process. You might consider emailing this to your leader as an opportunity for feedback.

3. If you have time, explore other places where the Bible describes how God receives those who mess up and turn back in repentance and faith. You might try Isaiah 54:4–8; Micah 7:18–20; and Luke 19:1–10.

TWENTY QUESTIONS TO DIAGNOSE YOUR HEART

We have looked at how our desires become demands and "needs." That is one way the Scriptures describe how our hearts go astray (Galatians 5:16–17; Ephesians 2:3). God has many other ways of describing what is going on inside us when we sin on the outside. Here are some questions to help you get at what's going on in your heart. They all start the same way: When I sin . . . .

1. What am I loving?

2. What am I seeking, aiming for, pursuing?

3. Where am I putting my hope?

4. What am I fearing? What do I not want? What am I worrying about?

5. Where am I looking for refuge, safety, and comfort?

6. What or whom am I trusting that is not the Lord?

7. Whose performance or control is making life work for me?

8. Whose opinion of me counts most? From whom do I desire approval and fear rejection?

9. What is making me feel rich, secure, and prosperous?

10. Whose victory or success am I hoping will make my life happy?

11. What am I thinking are my rights? What am I feeling entitled to?

12. What am I praying for?

13. What am I thinking about most? What preoccupies me? What am I obsessed with? In the morning, where does my mind instinctively drift?

14. What am I talking about? What is important to me? What attitudes am I communicating?

15. How am I spending my time?

16. What are my priorities?

17. What are my characteristic fantasies, either pleasurable or fearful? Daydreams? What do my night dreams revolve around?

18. What are my idols and false gods? In what do I place my trust or set my hopes? What do I turn to or seek? Where do I take refuge?

19. How do I implicitly say, "If only . . . " (to get what I want, avoid what I don't want, keep what I have)?

20. Where do I find my identity? How do I define who I am?

CROSS †

AIM

To help you reflect on the ways in which Jesus's mercies impact your past, present, and future.

RECAP

» God is working to change us.

» God is sovereign in every single kind of heat.

» We often respond from our hearts with bad fruit (thorns).

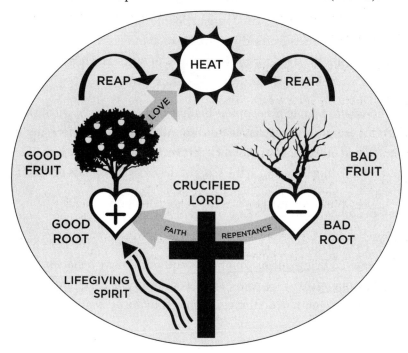

At this point in the course it's worth remembering a few things:

1. Thinking hard like this about our lives can feel uncomfortable and strange. Part of us really likes being the way we are, and we don't want to change (which is one big reason why, so far, we haven't!).

2. But God is at work in us. Change is his work, and it's a good work. We can trust him to do his work, and to do it in the best possible way. Taking his Word deeply to heart so we might worship him more is our privilege and our refuge in an uncertain world.

3. There are so many things that still need to change. Sin affects every area of our lives. To avoid feeling overwhelmed, and to think clearly during this course, it's best to pick just one thing to work on at a time, and follow where that leads.

DISCUSS

With your discussion partner, take a moment to pray about anything that seems important from your discussion.

Whatever the struggles of our heart, the solution can be found in Jesus. He is God and man. He came to show mercy to sinners and sufferers. He came to rescue us and not condemn us. While on earth, his life of mercy and truth embodied God's kingdom. He died in our place on the cross and rose from the dead for the forgiveness of our sins. He ascended to heaven, where he now reigns. He is alive forevermore!

His coronation gift to his people is his Spirit. Through his Spirit, he lives with his people and teaches us to respond to God as Father—loving him, loving others, and in every way growing to be more like him. He is now interceding for us, with the scars of the cross still on his body. One day he is going to return to wipe away every tear and bring us to a new heaven and new earth.

These wonderful truths affect every area of our lives. As the Holy Spirit enables us to bring our broken hearts and our thorny behavior to the Lord, through Christ we receive forgiveness for the past, hope for the future, and strength to do things differently in the present.

The word "cross" in the Three Trees diagram is intended to stand for all of this—for everything about our relationship with Christ, which is established in and focused on mercy and self-giving love, reaching its fullest expression on the cross of Christ.

CHRIST WINS OVER MY HEART

READ: COLOSSIANS 3:1-4

1. What has happened to us already, in the death and resurrection of Christ?

2. Where should our thoughts and dreams be focused now?

We have been raised (v. 1)! Christians don't just dream about a new life one day. We have one already, although it's still hidden (v. 3). And we have died (v. 3). The old self, committed to running away from God, has been replaced with a new one. This new life will be fully revealed in blazing glory one day when Christ appears (v. 4).

If we never think about this new life, we will find it feels rather empty and unexciting. Despite being real, it will wash over us and leave us unaffected. But if we "set our hearts" (v. 1) and "set our minds" (v. 2) on things above—on Christ who is reigning in glory at God's right hand (v. 1) and who will one day return—then our new life becomes our central priority and excitement. If we keep paying attention to Jesus (as Paul tells us in Colossians), the thought of living our new lives under his direction will consistently thrill us and encourage us to keep getting rid of behaviors belonging to our old life and to put on a new and far better wardrobe.

DISCUSS

Think about the issue you are working on. Tell your discussion partner how the truth of Colossians 3:1–4 affects the way you feel about that issue. What will you say to a partner who has been despairing, feeling stuck, or just feeling nothing?

Real change is truly possible, but how do we need to live day by day if this potential is to be realized?

I LIVE BY REPENTANCE AND FAITH IN JESUS

How should we respond to the wonderful truths that we have died with Christ and been raised with him? We respond in repentance and faith.

> » **Repentance** is about turning away from earth (our old self) and toward heaven—toward God. We need to discover what our hearts are really set on, earth or heaven.
>
> Ask: What earthly desires and preferences am I expressing at this point in my life? Where has God been pushed away, ignored, or replaced with a different priority? What must I turn from, and in what new direction will he lead me?

Then we put that into words addressed to God, in an act of sorrow and surrender from our heart.

> » **Faith** is about believing in the forgiveness of sins because of the cross of Christ, and trusting that, in Christ, the many promises of God hold me in relationship with God despite my sins.
>
> Ask: In a particular moment, which promises am I forgetting? What do I need to grasp again or grasp for the first time? If I am

stressed about a missed appointment, what does God promise that holds me, and every other part of the universe, stable and secure? If I feel defeated by sin, what promise will faith hold on to? And if I repent and acknowledge my sin before a holy God, how will he respond?

What does repentance and faith look like in a relationship? The parable of the lost son shows us.

READ: LUKE 15:11–32

3. What is the problem that took the younger son from his father? Why did he want to leave his father's house, with all it offered him?

4. How did he come to realize this was the problem?

5. What did he do when he realized this was the problem?

6. What does the story teach us about God's response when we repent?

The younger son had big problems in his heart (he thought satisfaction lay in wealth, fun, and independence) and he had major problems in his relationship with his father (he basically wanted him dead). He thought he was better off away from his father. But when he reached his lowest ebb, feeding the pigs, he realized he was far better off at home with his father. He returned in humility, confessing that his central offense had been relational, against heaven and his father.

The **essence of repentance** is to realize our sin is against God, and to turn back to him to ask for forgiveness for our treatment of him. We are called to bring our wrong desires and ungodly behavior to the Father in humble repentance. When the prodigal son returned, his father welcomed him with open arms. The **essence of faith** is to believe in our Father's love and forgiveness and to accept his loving embrace when we come back to him in repentance.

If we are going to repent of the many thorns we still have, we need to know for sure God will respond to us in the same way as the father in this story.

READ: 1 JOHN 1:9–10; 2:1–2; AND 3:1–3

7. From 1 John 1:9–10 and 2:1–2, how can we be sure God won't punish us for our sin if we admit it to him?

8. From 1 John 3:1–3, what relationship do we now have with God? What will the end result of this relationship be?

9. How does God's amazing love change the way you want to live now?

Jesus is at our side as we come before God. He reminds the Father of something he delights to hear, for it was all the Father's plan: Jesus has already taken the punishment we deserve. God chose to punish our sin in Jesus, so he cannot now punish it in us. That's guaranteed! We are God's precious children, loved beyond measure. One day our relationship with God will result in all sin being driven out. We will become like Jesus. Jesus is going to accomplish his work in us—there is no shadow of doubt. In the meantime, his Spirit gives us the insight and strength we need to keep turning toward him and away from our old life, where we lived for ourselves.

> No gloomy uncertainty as to God's favour can subdue one lust, or correct our crookedness of will. But the free pardon of the cross uproots sin, and withers all its branches. Only the certainty of love, forgiving love, can do this. Free and warm reception into the divine favour is the strongest of all motives in leading a man to seek conformity to Him who has thus freely forgiven him all trespasses. A cold admission into the paternal house by the father might have repelled the prodigal, and sent him back to his lusts; but the fervent kiss, the dear embrace, the best robe, the ring, the shoes, the fatted calf, the festal song—all without one moment's suspense or delay, as well as without one upbraiding word . . . . "Revellings, banquetings, and abominable idolatries" come to be the abhorrence of him round whom the holy arms of renewed fatherhood have been so lovingly thrown. Sensuality, luxury, and the gaieties of the flesh have lost their relish to one who has tasted the fruit of the tree of life.
>
> — HORATIUS BONAR[1]

LOOK AT YOUR OWN HEART

Think about the issue you are struggling with right now.

What could repentance and faith look like in the details of your own personal struggles? Can you say you are sorry now for both your thorns and the heart desires that drive them?

What is it about God and the new life he has given you in Christ that makes you want to turn away from your old ways, loves, desires, preferences, or fears?

---

1. Horatius Bonar, *The Everlasting Righteousness*, ed. Terry Kulakowski (Zeeland, MI: Reformed Church Publications, 2015), p. 88.

What greater, better, deeper desires or longings or possibilities does the gospel plant within you?

What confidence does the gospel give that you can live differently?

HOMEWORK

This week, spend a bit more time thinking about repentance and faith in this one area of your life. What aspects of the gospel seem most relevant to the longings and desires that are driving your behavior? What difference does the gospel make to your life? Forgiveness as you repent, for sure, but anything else? How does Jesus model perfection for you? What hope do you now have? Prayerfully keep aiming to understand this.

Next, consider what your life might look like as you begin to change. As your heart shifts in understanding, how could your life be different? What fruit might replace the thorns? How could things change for you and those close to you, and, in the process, how could this change affect your wider circumstances?

Write down some notes for yourself.

FRUIT

AIM

To help you reflect on the ways in which Jesus produces good fruit in your life.

RECAP

» Our Father is always working to change us.

» Our Father oversees every single moment (heat).

» We often respond from our complex hearts with bad fruit (thorns).

» The gospel of grace changes our hearts (cross).

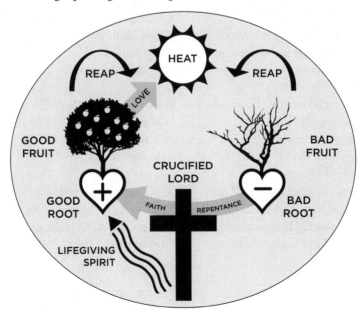

God is changing us in community, and he is active in every circumstance of our lives. We all have wayward hearts that respond wrongly to the pressures of life, but the gospel—the good news of Jesus's life, death, and resurrection—changes everything. As our hearts are changed, as we repent of our sinful desires and put our faith in God, we begin to bear good fruit. The good fruit we bear can be summed up by one word, "love." Growing love for God and people means we now can move into God's world in constructive, not destructive ways.

FRUIT COMES FROM A CHANGED HEART

The famous hymn writer John Newton recorded a little of his process of change—from slave ship captain to child of God—in his music. Newton's most famous hymn is "Amazing Grace," but one other hymn is called "In Evil Long I Took Delight." Take a few moments to reflect on the words:

In evil long I took delight,
Unawed by shame or fear,
Till a new object struck my sight,
And stopped my wild career.

I saw One hanging on a tree,
In agonies and blood,
Who fixed His loving eyes on me,
As near His cross I stood.

Sure, never till my latest breath,
Can I forget that look;
It seemed to charge me with His death,
Though not a word He spoke.

My conscience felt and owned the guilt,
And plunged me in despair,
I saw my sins His blood had spilt,
And helped to nail Him there.

Alas, I knew not what I did,
But now my tears are vain;
Where shall my trembling soul be hid?
For I the Lord have slain.

A second look He gave, which said,
"I freely all forgive;
This blood is for thy ransom paid;
I die that thou mayst live."

Thus, while His death my sin displays
In all its blackest hue,
Such is the mystery of grace,
It seals my pardon too.

With pleasing grief and mournful joy,
My spirit is now filled;
That I should such a life destroy,
Yet live by him I killed.

REFLECT

1. What stopped John Newton's "wild career?" How have you seen this happen in your life as a Christian?

2. Are there other hymns or songs about the cross that move you in a similar way?

3. As you think about your change project, based on what you have learned in this course, which of the following have you done in the past? Describe your goal for change now.

   » Continuing as you are, responding in the same ways, with no change

   » Trying to change your behavior so you respond in better ways next time

   » Growing closer to Jesus, being more passionate about him, and responding more like him day by day

DISCUSS

Describe to your discussion partner how you feel about each of these three options.

4. Which of the above will actually happen in your case? How can you be certain (Philippians 1:6)? How do you feel about that?

As we freshly experience God's love and grace for our sin, our desires for ourselves pale beside a growing desire to be like Christ. The Spirit of God takes the Word of God as it proclaims the Son of God crucified and raised and presses it into our hearts as the growing object of our supreme desire. Increasingly we will be able to say with the apostle Paul, "I want to know Christ—yes, to know the power of his resurrection and participation in his sufferings, becoming like him in his death, and so, somehow, attaining to the resurrection from the dead. Not that I have already obtained all this, or have already arrived at my goal, but I press on to take hold of that for which Christ Jesus took hold of me" (Philippians 3:10–12).

READ: TITUS 2:11–14

Verses 13 and 14 are the driving force, not the explanatory footnote. We live every moment now as a people-in-waiting for something amazing: our hearts are changed, and we are increasingly "eager to do what is good."

5. In what ways are you eager to do good as you reflect again on what God has done and is doing in you?

BY GRACE I CAN BEAR THE FRUIT OF CHRISTLIKENESS

READ: GALATIANS 5:16–6:10

The Galatian church was in trouble because people were teaching that keeping certain laws could improve their standing with the God of all grace. Paul responds by explaining that grace sets us free from such burdens and by showing how real freedom should be used.

6. See if you can use a biblical lens to understand the struggle the Galatians were facing by identifying their heat, thorns, cross (gospel hope), and fruit. You might like to annotate the following diagram:

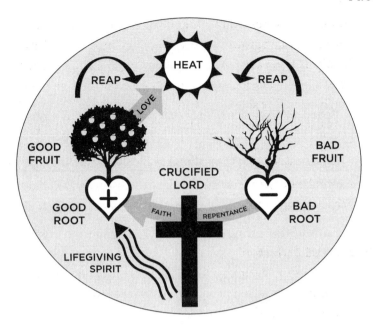

The Galatians were facing false teaching and conflict. They were responding with drunkenness, impurity, envy, and all kinds of fighting—all flowing out of hearts that were proud of how law-abiding they were. The good news, however, is that they belonged to Jesus, and their wrong desires had already been put to death. By following the Spirit's lead, they would grow the wonderful fruit of becoming like Jesus.

If change can happen in the Galatian church, it can happen in us! Each time we act in ungodly ways, we can be alert to our thorns, conscious of our wayward desires, eager to repent, keen to remind ourselves that we are forgiven, called to something better, and committed to responding to the grace we have received by acting in radically loving ways, spurred on by our brothers and sisters in Christ. This is utterly thrilling!

REFLECT

Pick an aspect of the Spirit's fruit described here that seems particularly relevant to the issue you are considering during this course.

> » **Love**: Caring about God and others more than yourself, seen in the following . . . .

» **Joy**: Unshakable delight that God is about his good work always

» **Peace**: Deep-seated confidence that, even when it seems otherwise, and even in great pain, nothing is out of control, and you are safe in God's hands

» **Patience**: Waiting in faith in every situation and relationship for God to glorify Christ and fulfill his purpose in his perfect timing

» **Kindness**: Acting toward others in such a way that they may enjoy what is truly good

» **Goodness**: Doing what is right and beautiful before God

» **Faithfulness**: Living each moment in a responsive, trusting relationship with God

» **Gentleness**: Responding without temper, mindful that the other is frail and weak like you

» **Self-control**: Doggedly resisting temptation to do anything other than all the above

» **Such things**: Paul opens the door to other fruit of the Spirit by saying, "Against such things there is no law" (Galatians 5:23). So you can pick an aspect of the Spirit's work not listed here, such as honesty, integrity, courage, or encouragement.

Imagine this fruit ripening in your life! How would your life be different? What would you be thinking/feeling/doing in the heat of life? What would you be finding hard? How would you be overcoming those hard things? How would this fruit affect the people around you? What will help this fruit grow?

The good news of the gospel is this fruit grows and goes on growing. Don't be satisfied until you have it, but grow patience while you are waiting for the fruit to appear!

HOMEWORK

1. The kind of change we are talking about does not start with this course. To explore how God has already been at work in you, consider a part of Scripture that has been significant in your life.

Take a moment to write it out here.

What has made it so significant? For example, what does it say about God? What does it say about you? How does it speak to your heart and the desires that live there? How has it changed you from within? How has that affected your relationship with God or encouraged you to live differently with others?

2. In our session this week, you thought about what change will look like as the fruit of the Spirit grows where once there were thorns. How will your heart need to be different for this to happen? (Remember, we are not just looking for your actions to change!)

How does the gospel make this change possible and desirable?

Now ask God for help to watch yourself this week in the pressure points of your heat. What is happening? If things are not as different as you want them to be, where will you focus? How does the gospel provide hope in the moments of failure? Are you learning anything else about your thorns and the heart from which they come? If things seem to be different, why is this? Write down your thoughts.

session

6 REAL CHANGE

AIM

To help you persevere in a lifelong journey of change with your eyes firmly fixed on Jesus.

RECAP

» Our Father is always working to change us in Christ. In the midst of our sufferings, he engages our sins with his mercy in order to transform us.

» We face many hardships, losses, trials and temptations (heat).

» We often respond from our complex hearts with bad fruit (thorns).

» The gospel of grace changes our hearts (cross).

» We are enabled to respond with beautiful fruit, to the praise of his grace (fruit).

As Philippians 1:6 reminds us, "He who began a good work in you will carry it on to completion until the day of Christ Jesus" (ESV).

DISCUSS

Summarize the issue you have been considering throughout this course. Describe:

» HEAT: The situation in or to which I am responding

» THORNS: My sinful responses and the consequences that are reaped

» HEART: What lies underneath these responses in my heart

» CROSS: The gospel as it connects with my heart, my fears, my idols, my misplaced desires, my goods-made-gods, etc.

» HEART: What I'm repenting of; what new desires are in my heart

» FRUIT: What it will look like to live according to these new desires, and the consequences that may follow

You may want to make brief notes on the Three Trees diagram.

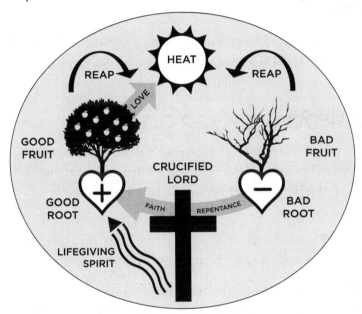

WHAT DOES REAL CHANGE LOOK LIKE?

It's important to clarify four things about real change.

» Real change means actual fruit in your life (Matthew 3:8; 2 Corinthians 7:10). Wanting to change in new ways is a crucial step, but we haven't really changed until we've really changed!

» Real change is usually slow growing (2 Corinthians 3:18). God completes his work over a lifetime, and while some things can change quickly, we often grow the additional precious fruit of patience or endurance while we change more slowly than we want.

» Real change is only complete when we see Jesus face-to-face (1 John 3:2). There will always be room for more repentance and faith, learning to honor Christ in fresh ways, so we will continue to live with thorns in ourselves and others.

» Real change is always possible (Philippians 1:6). Since all the power of God's Spirit is at work in all God's children, we are never truly stuck where we are.

DISCUSS

Which of the above statements do you need to remember most?

HOW DO WE KEEP GOING?

Over the past six sessions, you have started to address an issue in your life. You will need to keep going with this issue, and there will be other facets of your life to address. What will help you do that?

REFLECT

In this course you have experienced several approaches:

» Bible: Reading and carefully studying God's Word

» Prayer: Telling God all about your struggles and asking him for help

» The Three Trees model: Getting to the heart of what motivates your actions

» Conversation: Discussing our lives in the light of the Bible with honesty and love

» Accountability: Checking in with consistent groups

» Structure: Meeting over a number of weeks

» Writing: Noting key areas of challenge or growth

DISCUSS

Which of these approaches have you found most useful? (Pick three or four.) Which of these are available outside this course? Which are already in place? Which others could usefully be arranged?

This kind of thinking and praying is meant to be a normal part of church life. Church is more than a place of personal change, but it should never be less than a place of change.

THIS IS REAL CHURCH!

Think back to the last sermon you heard, the last Bible study you attended (small group or one to one), and/or the last quiet time you had. Think about what the Scriptures you considered say about the struggle you have been focusing on during this course.

What did God teach you through his Word in the following:

> » Your last sermon?

> » Your last time of worship?

> » Your last time you received the Lord's Supper?

> » Your last small group?

» Your last opportunity to discuss the Bible with someone individually?

» Your last personal reading?

We can't expect every worship time, sermon, communion, and Bible study to speak directly to the specific concerns that are highest in our minds at any given time—the Bible does not serve our agenda. But we should expect God to address us through his living Word. In all the above, the key is to think seriously about your walk with God. Keep asking yourself not just about your actions but ask questions like this:

How is my relationship with God right now?

Who is God to me, and how am I relating to him?

What am I learning about him that helps shape my response to him?

Is repentance and faith a normal part of everyday life, or has it stalled?

How will the gospel restart this critical dynamic at the heart of all real change?

DISCUSS

It is helpful to plan how to make the most of the opportunities for growth in your church. Consider the following strategies. Which are likely to be most useful to you in growing in love for God and others?

» I'm going to try to talk about the sermon, and how it connected with me, with someone after church.

» In my small group, I'm going to share a prayer request that asks God to change my heart rather than only asking him to change my circumstances.

» I'm going to keep a journal of what I am learning in Bible study and how it applies to my desires.

» I am going to start reading the Bible with someone and make myself accountable for some of the things I'm struggling with.

» I am going to notice others who are acting graciously and courageously and remember to encourage them and be thankful for them.

» I am going to notice the world God has made—its beauty, detail, and the way he clothes the lilies of the field and watches over the sparrows. I will remember to share my gratitude for creation with others around me.

Remember that, just as you are greatly helped by interactions with others, God also makes you helpful to others. Just as you are encouraged to see God more clearly and hold to him more nearly, so you can encourage others in the same way. How can the things you've experienced in this course be used to bless others?

REFLECT

It's good to celebrate the fruit you have seen in your life over the past six sessions (however large or small it might have been), praising God for his work in you. As you look back over this course, what sticks out for you on a personal level? What are you thankful for? What are you prayerful about?

One great result of this course would be to have a greater sense of need for God to work in your heart in some specific way. In what ways do you think your heart might be undergoing change at the moment? What has God been working on with you? Are there any signs of fruit? How do you feel about that?

Talk about this with your discussion partner and spend some time in prayer.

> "And we all, who with unveiled faces contemplate the Lord's glory, are being transformed into his image with ever-increasing glory, which comes from the Lord, who is the Spirit" (2 Corinthians 3:18).

HOMEWORK

Write a page tracking yourself around the Three Trees, building on what you have written before. You can send this to the course leader in the next couple of weeks along with a plan of action for continued growth, confident that it is good and godly to keep pursuing real change!

FEEDBACK

NAME:
(OPTIONAL UNLESS YOU WANT A RESPONSE!)

Something good I am taking away from the course is:

Something I don't understand or want to hear more about is:

Something to think about for running the course better is:

The general issue I have been thinking about during the course is:

One way in which I might use what I have been learning for others is:

REAL CHANGE
LEADER'S GUIDE

INTRODUCTION

This *Leader's Guide* is designed to help you lead participants through the biblical process of change. Along the way you will be challenged, encouraged, and helped as well. That's how the Spirit works! This introduction contains the information you need to prepare for leading your group.

WHO IS THE COURSE FOR?

Whether we are new Christians or mature Christians, we all have areas of our lives that need transforming. Some of us lean toward anger or impatience, others toward jealousy or discontent. Some of us struggle with addictions and, in different ways, all of us still harbor pride in our hearts. God is not planning on leaving us this way! As Paul reminds us, he is going to bring to completion the good work he has already begun in us (Philippians 1:6). But how does this process of change work? *Real Change* is a course for anyone who wants to find out how the gospel changes us from the inside out—anyone who wants to take a look at what is going on in his or her heart and grow with God's help to see real change. That means it is suitable for both new Christians who want to discover more about change and more mature Christians who may know the principles but still value having a structure in which to pursue that change.

HOW CAN THE COURSE BE USED?

The course is designed to be used within a local church (or other grouping of Christians). It can be used with groups as small as four or groups as large as forty, but the ideal size is probably in the region of ten to twenty. It is a course designed to be led from the front. That means you or someone you assign will need to lead each week, giving biblical input and facilitating discussion.

WHAT DOES THE COURSE CONTAIN?

The course contains six sessions, each taking about an hour and a half. Each week builds on the one that comes before it, so it is important that participants aim to come to all six sessions. It's important that the leaders are there for all the sessions too!

The course is based on CCEF's "Three Trees" diagram and CCEF's own, longer course, Dynamics of Biblical Change.

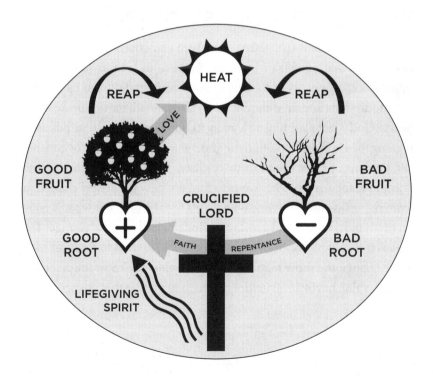

The Three Trees diagram is a simple representation of how change happens, inspired by Jeremiah 17:5–8. It takes seriously that we all live in the world surrounded by pressures from hard things that can stress us and good things that can distract us (the "heat"). Sometimes we respond to that heat by behaving in ways that dishonor Jesus ("thorns / bad fruit"). This is because the desires of our hearts are ungodly or we over desire things that are good (that's the "bad root"). This ungodly behavior in turn negatively influences what is going on around us (this is what is meant by "reap"). But there is a way for this to change! As God, by grace, draws us back, to *constantly* return to Jesus in repentance and faith (the "cross"), we begin to have our heart desires transformed so we want what he wants (this is the "good root"). As the good root grows through the Spirit's work, so our behavior changes to be more Christlike ("good fruit"). This has a wonderfully positive impact on the world around us ("reap"). This is how the Bible describes change, and it's a picture infused with grace and hope.

This model of change runs throughout the course, so it is worth spending time understanding it before you begin leading any sessions. This model is not intended to supersede Scripture but to summarize Scripture. Please use the model in such a way that it encourages people to run toward the Bible rather than seeing it as a stand-alone model.

HOW DO I RUN THE COURSE?

We encourage you to enter into your preparation prayerfully and diligently. The course deals with people's hearts and lives, and that is not something to be taken lightly.

PREPARING YOUR HEART

Before preparing the material, it is important to prepare your heart. It can be tempting, as a leader, to go to one of two extremes:

> »   "I'm sorted out and I'm going to tell others how to get their lives together too."

» "I'm a hypocritical worm. There's no way I should be leading a course like this!"

Neither is helpful! We are all sinners saved by grace and in need of change. You and the participants are walking this journey of grace together. To that end, it is going to be important to set aside time to pray for yourself and your participants' hearts. It will also help the participants to hear you reflect at times on how you have been learning and growing, with a bit of gritty detail. Leading means being ready to do this, for their sake and God's glory.

PREPARING THE MATERIAL

Each week you will teach a new aspect of the Three Trees diagram, facilitate some discussion on the biblical basis and application of that aspect, and then assign some "homework" to help the participants put into action what they have been learning.

THE THREE TREES

The teaching on the Three Trees diagram will take place from the front. You may want to use PowerPoint or flip charts to help you along. The teaching slots are relatively short, so please don't feel you need to prepare lengthy talks. (If you do, you will run out of time!)

Throughout each session are questions for participants to answer. The questions are numbered and suggested answers and helps are included with the question number in this *Leader's Guide*. Each section also has a suggested time frame to help you cover all the material from each session in ninety minutes. "Links" are also included, giving you ideas on how to move from one section to another throughout each session. Another important element is time for prayer—since change happens as we ask the Spirit to help us. The times don't add up to ninety minutes in all, so you still have some flexibility in how much time you spend on discussion, linking each section together, and prayer.

DISCUSSION

Some of the discussion time will take place as a whole group, but much of the discussion will take place with a discussion partner. The idea is that people will sit with the same discussion partner each week and begin a relationship that really embodies Hebrews 10:24: one that spurs one another on to love and good works. Once you know who your participants will be, think through who might work with whom. Single gender pairs tend to be best. Some group leaders choose to put people in groups of three instead of two, making it easier to cope with one person missing a week. However, doing this will also make the discussion times longer than the times suggested in this guide, and it will be harder to finish each evening within ninety minutes.

HOMEWORK

The homework will revolve around a personal change project. Each participant will be asked to identify one area of his or her life that is not as it should be and begin to work on it. Given that the course is only six weeks, it's probably wise for participants to choose a smaller issue. Each week, they will discuss their thoughts with their discussion partners. There are also two points in the course where participants will be encouraged to email you as the course leader to let you know what they are learning about themselves and how they are changing. These emails are to be encouraged as it keeps people accountable and gives you, as the leader, the opportunity to encourage, inspire, and (when appropriate) invite people to chat individually with you. You are not asked to "mark" this homework, merely to use it as an opportunity to encourage. Occasionally in courses like this, serious pastoral problems rear their heads, and it is important to be willing to step in where necessary or refer elsewhere as needed.

PREPARING THE LOGISTICS

Before the course begins, make sure you work through this checklist:

- » Have I booked a venue?
- » Have I advertised the course details / invited participants? (And had the replies?)

» Have I ordered the appropriate number of study guides?

» Have I got an ample supply of Bibles for people to use?

» Have I got enough pens for people to use?

» Have I arranged to have a flip chart and pens / computer and projector ready?

» Am I going to record each session? It's very helpful for people who have to miss a session to catch up. If so, have I got the microphones and recording equipment ready?

» Have I worked through the Leader's Guide and understood the model?

» Have I made time to read and respond to participants' emails?

» Am I going to provide refreshments at the start of the session? (Refreshment time will need to be **in addition** to the hour and a half needed for each session.)

» Have I thought about how the group can divide into pairs?

» Have I liaised with the participants to let them know what the course is going to involve?

PREPARING THE PARTICIPANTS

Once participants have expressed interest in the course, email them to say you are looking forward to welcoming them at *Real Change* and stressing the need to be there every week (unless sudden illness or trauma hits). Please let them know they are going to be asked to take part in a personal change project that you hope is going to be exciting, useful, and thoroughly biblically based. Also encourage them to remember this is a six-session course, so they need to have realistic expectations of how much they will change in that time—lives rarely transform dramatically in a few short weeks. The purpose of the course is to encourage a process of change that will, for all of us, continue until Jesus returns or he calls us home. You can tell participants a little of how the course will work, and make sure they know to expect some modest "homework," with matters to reflect on and write down at various points. Invite them to contact you with any concerns. Courses like this can sometimes be very appealing to the most fragile members of a congregation, so it's a good idea to consider what extra support such people may need.

SESSION 1: CHANGE

AIM

To help participants reflect on the need for change and the certainty of change. To provide a brief overview of the process of change.

WELCOME *(10 MINUTES)*

It's the first session of a new course, and participants will be feeling a range of emotions. Some will be excited, others nervous, a few wondering why on earth they came! It's good to spend a little time reminding participants of why they are here, what's going to happen, and what success looks like. You might like to cover points like these:

> » This course is about change and becoming more conscious of God's transforming work in us.

> » This course is not about the giving of theoretical information; it's about seeing God's Word working practically in our lives.

> » This course isn't a race. Humans tend to change slowly. There will be no perfection in six weeks! The process of transformation is designed by God to last a lifetime.

> » This course will be a success if we change, if we start to change, or if we become more aware of the need of change.

> » This course is divided into six sessions each designed to last 1.5 hours. Part of the time we will be listening, much of the time we will be chatting in (same gender) pairs.

> » This course will be a safe place. What we share here should not be shared with anyone else.

> » This course contains homework after each session (which will take about an hour). If you get stuck, people are welcome to email the course leader.

> » This course requires regular attendance, and it would be great if everyone could be on time!

Much of the discussion in this course will be taking place in pairs, with discussion partners. If your group knows one another well, you can simply ask them to get into pairs at the start of this session. If your group doesn't know one another well—or if there are particular sensitivities within the group of which to be aware—you might want to assign partners. It is good practice to encourage people of the same gender to work together. From experience, couples who have been married a few years can find it hard to "shift gears" to talk at a heart level together if they are not used to it. Asking married couples to pair with someone of their own gender, and to share with their spouse what they are learning afterward, avoids this awkwardness and helps them get the most from the course.

PRAY

As you begin the session, turn to the Lord in prayer. Thank him for being gracious and kind, and ask him to be working in everyone's lives.

LIVES IN NEED OF CHANGE *(15 MINUTES)*

Read aloud (or have a participant read) the first part of the case study to get people thinking and chatting about struggles. Then allow the participants four or five minutes to consider the first set of "**reflect**" questions. You might like to say you are looking for honest answers, not the "right" answers. *(5 MINUTES)*

People will come up with a range of answers, including guilt, anxiety, anger, despair, or the sense that life is out of control. Some people may be completely unflustered by such events (though probably not many!). Encourage people to share their responses briefly. Don't be afraid of asking follow-up questions too. If someone says he would be feeling angry, ask who he would be angry at: himself, his mother, the friend who didn't answer the phone, or God? You might ask why someone is feeling angry too. Try to keep this section light. We don't want anyone to feel condemned by others in the room. We are all sinners with the capacity to react negatively when the stress piles up.

Read the next part of the case study and encourage the group to **reflect** on the next set of questions. *(3-5 MINUTES)*

Begin by asking what people's initial reactions to this scenario would be. Give them just a few seconds to think. Would they put their plans on hold? Would they rush off without spending time with their tearful friend because they are late? Would they offer a casual, "It'll be fine"? Would they see her needs as greater or lesser than theirs? The idea is not to find the right answer but to see the varied responses that can come from the human heart.

Next, ask what a more considered response could be. Participants may come up with a whole array of answers but common ones include: offering to pray for the friend, arranging to meet up the next day, and reminding the friend of a great truth about God. Some might notice God had clearly intended you to meet your friend at just that moment, experiencing very similar stress as you do.

You might follow up this discussion by asking, "What truths about God would you want your friend to know?" Think of ways we can briefly remind others in the midst of stress that God is loving, sovereign, trustworthy, and kind. *(5 MINUTES)*

LINK

This course is going to help us move away from our old self (with all its selfish desires) and put on our new self (with all its kingdom values) and we are going to be looking at the process little by little.

Here you might give a brief overview of the course. Point people to the structure at the front of their study guides and give them an opportunity to ask any questions they might have about the journey ahead.

LIVES IN A CONTEXT OF CHANGE *(2 MINUTES)*

It's time to begin the process of change! How better to begin than by asking people to consider how they would like to change? Allow people two minutes to discuss that question with their discussion partner.

There probably isn't any need to ask for feedback on this question. Some things shared will have been very private and inappropriate to share more widely. Simply encourage people to keep their answers in mind, open their Bibles, and prepare to discover how we can be confident that change really is possible.

GOD IS CHANGING EACH OF US

(10 MINUTES)

Read 2 Corinthians 3:18, then allow five minutes for participants to **discuss** the two questions with their discussion partner.

1. Here it is good to draw out that change is a work of the Spirit. And, because it is God who is doing the work, change is definitely going to happen!

2. We are being transformed to be ever more like Jesus, changed into God's image. Of course, we are already in God's image (Genesis 1 teaches us that) but that image has been marred by sin. We are being remade day by day, and that should be an exciting prospect (though other emotions may be present too!).

LINK

Ask for feedback on each of the questions. For some people, these will be familiar truths; for others this will be a whole new way of thinking.

It is likely that at least some people in the group will be thinking, "But why would Jesus bother with me?" Ask the group to imagine a run-down house. Some people might pass by and think, "What a wreck!" but others might see its potential and think, "One day this will be beautiful." God is like the person who sees the potential beauty. He knows how broken we are, but he also knows what we will one day become as he works in us.

So, confident that change is not just possible but a present reality, we can begin looking more at the relationships involved in change. It is worth reminding participants that we all have a vertical relationship (with God) and horizontal relationships (with others). Both are important in the process of transformation.

GOD IS CHANGING US THROUGH OUR RELATIONSHIP WITH JESUS

(15 MINUTES)

Note how people see their relationship with Jesus. The way we view Jesus will impact our view of how he is going to change us. A number of biblical metaphors are valid, so hopefully most of the group will draw on these. Some people may share unbiblical models. Handle these gently. Encourage them to reframe their thinking in a more biblical way and perhaps invite them to chat with you afterwards.

READ: EPHESIANS 1:1–14

3. See if your group can pick up on the repeated use of "in Christ" / "united with Christ."

4. Being united with Christ brings all of these metaphors together and give us even more! This is wonderfully exciting! It means all the blessings Christ deserves are blessings given to us. It means his identity is now our identity.

5. We get to be holy and blameless, fully redeemed. God will be praised forever for his glorious grace in choosing and transforming us to live under Christ's rule.

Ask for feedback on the questions. There are some complex pictures here. Try not to get drawn into peripheral details. Try to stay focused on the big picture: that our precious, uniting relationship with Jesus is at the center of our transformation.

In our individualistic society, it can be easy to think that the method of change simply requires one-on-one time with Jesus, but it is a far more corporate process. Ask group members to read the next passage and answer the question below.

GOD IS CHANGING US THROUGH OUR RELATIONSHIPS WITH OTHER CHRISTIANS *(5–10 MINUTES)*

READ: EPHESIANS 4:11-16

and have participants discuss with their discussion partner.

6. God effects change in us, but we also change as we speak the truth in love to one another and build one another up. We need one another, and the words we say matter for our growth.

Church is so much more than sermons and songs. Every interaction we have with other believers has the potential to help us grow.

A MODEL FOR UNDERSTANDING CHANGE *(20 MINUTES)*

Read Jeremiah 17:5–8 aloud. This passage is the basis for the model of change that we will use throughout this course. Then briefly introduce the participants to the overall process of change and the diagram that is going to undergird the rest of the sessions. It is worth drawing this section by section on a flip chart or chalkboard (and doing so confident that it will be helpful even if you can't draw well!). As you draw each section, provide one-sentence summaries of each concept, and link back to the case study at the start (briefly). Here are some possible one-sentence summaries to use:

1. The **Heat**: Things that happen to us (both good and bad) that put us under pressure.

2. **Root/Heart**: The place (the Bible calls this our heart, soul, mind, will) where we decide how we are going to respond to what is going on around us and to God.

3. **Thorns**: The self-focused, not God-focused, ways we respond to the heat of life (like being angry with people who take "our" parking slot).

4. **Reap** (negative consequences): Our decision to respond in a self-focused way negatively affects our relationships and the situations we are in.

5. **Lifegiving Spirit**: The Spirit meets us in our sinfulness, helps us to repent at the foot of the cross, emboldens our faith, and then brings about change in our hearts and lives.

6. **Cross**: This represents all the things God reveals about himself through Jesus's death and resurrection. We are connected to Christ through the work of the Spirit in repentance and faith. All change happens in relationship to Christ and his cross.

7. **Good root**: As we go to Jesus every day, our roots go down deep into him, and our desires, thoughts, and actions gradually change to be like him.

8. **Good fruit**: These are the God-honoring ways we can respond to the heat of life.

9. **Reap** (positive consequences): When we respond to our heat in Christ, the result is good fruit—you will be blessed and be a blessing to others.

It doesn't matter if group members don't quite get this on the first session. It will become clearer as the weeks go on. They should at least be able to grasp that there are different ways of responding to situations and we want to respond more and more like Jesus as time goes on. That change happens as we, together, return time and again to the cross.

If there is time, you can encourage them to look again at the case study used at the start. Can they fit each element into the heat-thorns-cross-fruit structure?

CHANGE HOMEWORK

At the end of the session, introduce the participants to the homework for this week, reading through that section with them, and give them the chance to ask any questions they might have.

If people need ideas for what area of their lives to pick, you might use some of these examples:

- » Your driving habits
- » The way you play golf (or other competitive sport)
- » Your relationship to money and possessions
- » Your tendency to misuse comforts and pleasures
- » Anxiety
- » Sex and romance
- » Fear of people
- » Your broken or strained relationships
- » Any tendency to become self-absorbed
- » How you relate to authority
- » Response to being sinned against
- » Patterns of work and rest
- » Temptation to grumble

SESSION 2: HEAT

AIM

To help participants reflect on the ways in which their circumstances impact their heart and to enable them to begin their journey of change.

DURING THE WEEK

It can be helpful to email people during the week to remind them of their homework, to let them know how to access the recording of the first session (if you've made one) and to encourage them that the process of change is going to be worthwhile. Please make sure you spend some time praying for the participants prior to this second session.

WELCOME *(10 MINUTES)*

At the start of the session, welcome everyone back to the course and encourage them to sit with their discussion partner. Once everyone is settled, read Jeremiah 17:5–15. You might like to sketch in a little context: the people of Judah had sinned and God punished them by sending them into exile in Babylon. This passage is part of his subsequent message of hope.

PRAY

As you begin the session, turn to the Lord in prayer. You might like to ask for his help to acknowledge that our hearts need help and thank him for this opportunity to grow.

RECAP

Hopefully most people will remember what happened last week, but it's useful to give a very short recap. It will be particularly helpful to remind everyone that they are designed for relationship with God and with one another—and that God, who has begun his good work in us, has promised to bring it to completion.

HEAT – THORNS – CROSS – FRUIT

READ: JEREMIAH 17:5-15 *(10 MINUTES)*

Have the group look again at the diagram that was introduced last week. Briefly go over the model, pointing out the need to grow by moving from a place where we respond from our own sinful desires to a place where we trust God more by being transformed by the gospel.

The process of change outlined in the diagram can seem quite long. There may be people in the group who want to simplify matters and suggest that it's possible to simply use self-control and do things differently. So it's important to say that this course is not just about behavior change but about heart change. You might find the "fruit stapling" illustration useful here, borrowed from Paul Tripp[1]: Imagine you have an apple tree. Each year it bears beautiful apples. But there is a problem; you don't like apples, you like pears. One day you come up with an ingenious plan. You remove all the apples from the tree and staple loads of pears onto the branches instead. For a few short days you can look out of your window and see a beautiful tree laden in pears. For a little while you can go into your garden and pick a ripe, juicy pear. But it doesn't last. The next year, you're back to square one. The tree bears nothing but apples. Behavior change is a bit like fruit stapling. Exercising self-control can bring out a different way of acting for a while but it's not a long-term solution, because the person hasn't really changed. Real change means looking at the heart, and that takes time. You can refer back to Jeremiah 17 again here and stress that, as humans, we often look to quick-fix solutions, but real, beautiful change only comes from the Lord as we learn to be rooted in him and love like he does.

REFLECTION *(15 MINUTES)*

Encourage the group to **reflect** on the ways in which the first part of the diagram (the heat) relates to their own life. Ask them to share with their discussion partners the ways in which life is hard or joyful (heat includes both the positives and negatives of life). And, in particular, encourage them to share what they observed about themselves as they did their

---

1. Paul David Tripp, *Instruments in the Redeemer's Hands* (Philipsburg, NJ: P&R, 2002) 63–65

homework. Allow each person in the pair just three minutes to share. This will encourage short insights rather than life-stories to be passed on. Then allow an extra two minutes for each partner to ask any questions of clarification. Once each partner has had an opportunity to share, allow another couple of minutes for each person to write a summary sentence outlining their partner's heat.

LINK

Things that are discussed in pairs don't need to be shared more widely with the group, but you might like to ask participants how they found the process of sharing. Some people may have found it a frustratingly short amount of time in which to share their heat. Others may be feeling uncomfortable talking about themselves for so long.

It's good to understand each other's heat, but it's even more important to remember that God understands our situations completely and is changing us in them.

GOD UNDERSTANDS MY SITUATION

READ: PSALM 22:1-19 *(10 MINUTES)*
Allow a few minutes for the participants to look at the questions with their discussion partners. Ask for feedback and, as comments flow, draw out that the psalmist is pointing to the depths of Jesus's suffering on the cross. God doesn't just understand in an academic way; he truly knows the depths of pain.

LINK

God doesn't just understand; the hard times we experience are all part of his good and sovereign plan. He has a high purpose for us, one that we might not understand now but which is ultimately good for us.

READ: 1 PETER 1:3-9 *(10 MINUTES)*
Allow a few minutes for participants to answer the questions with their discussion partners.

2. Ask for some feedback and encourage people to appreciate that heat, while often painful, is faith-refining—and that is both good for us and something that brings glory to Christ.

3. Rather than asking God to take away our trials, we can ask him to change us to be more like Jesus in them.

4. Peter uses the image of fire (heat!). We have hope because the fire doesn't consume our faith—it purifies it.

LINK

By this stage of the session, the participants will hopefully be grasping that the heat of our life really can make things desperately hard, but the heat is not pointless. We're going to explore that next by looking at how the Israelites responded to their experiences in the desert. It will be necessary to move through these Bible passages fairly quickly.

GOD ENABLES ME TO GROW IN RESPONSE TO MY SITUATION

READ: NUMBERS 11:4-15 *(5 MINUTES)*
5. The Israelites forgot the horrors of Egypt and thought that God had brought them into the desert to die. They grumbled repeatedly and thought they were better off as slaves.

READ: DEUTERONOMY 8:2-3 *(5 MINUTES)*
6. Try to draw out the fact that God wanted what was best for the Israelites. He was humbling them, teaching them dependence, and showing them that life is most importantly about trusting God's promises.

READ: 1 CORINTHIANS 10:1-11 *(20 MINUTES)*
7. The Israelites' experiences are also designed to teach us! Their experiences remind us that God isn't some kind of killjoy but a good God who longs to make us holy in an ever-deeper relationship with him.

There are huge depths in these passages. You won't be able to explore them thoroughly, but allow the participants a few minutes to share what they have been discovering. Then it is time to move on to what is maybe the most important part of the session: reframing our struggles in the light of God's good purposes for us. Get people back with their discussion partners, and encourage them to **read** the sentence they wrote earlier about their partners' struggles and check with their partners that they have understood their situations accurately. Then, with the above Bible verses in mind, ask them to **reframe** their sentence so it includes more of God's purposes for the suffering. Read with the group the examples in the study guide. Participants clearly don't know every facet of their partners' struggles after only a short conversation, and they won't know every facet of the mind of God either, so it is good to encourage humility in these sentences. But there are also some glorious truths about which we can be confident—God is good and he is active!

LINK

The above exercise will have shown that, even in some painful circumstances, God's good purposes are at work. The tough times aren't cause for despair but cause for hope that we can and will become more like Jesus. But before we get on to the fruit, we need to be real about the unhelpful ways we tend to respond to heat: our thorns. The final task of the evening is to explain this week's homework.

CHANGE HOMEWORK

The idea is to encourage people to be attentive to how they are really reacting when the pressure is on—in thought, word, and deed. You might like to encourage them to jot down what they observe about themselves this week. They do not need to slavishly answer every question written in the guide but, rather, use the questions as a framework to help them notice how they are behaving when the heat is on.

PRAY

As the session ends, spend a little while thanking God for his good plans for us and for the opportunities to change to be more like Jesus.

SESSION 3: THORNS

AIM

To help participants reflect on the ways in which the desires of their hearts drive their responses to the heat of life.

DURING THE WEEK

It can be helpful to email people during the week to remind them of their homework, to let them know how to access the recordings of the first two sessions (if you've made them), and to encourage them that the process of change is going to be worthwhile. Please make sure you spend some time praying for the participants as you prepare for this third session.

WELCOME AND PRAYER

At the start of the session, welcome everyone back to the course and encourage them to sit with their discussion partner. As you begin, remind people that things shared in the room will stay in the room (unless life-threatening or legally reportable issues are shared) and then turn to the Lord in prayer. You might like to acknowledge the waywardness of the human heart and thank God for his promise to complete the work he has started in each of us.

GETTING STARTED

Hopefully, most people will remember what happened last week but it's useful to give a very short recap. Remind people that God is changing us, and he is never going to change his mind and stop that work. You can also remind participants that God changes each of us in the situations we are in; we don't need life to calm down before we begin to change. He is using our circumstances, the people around us, and our relationship with him to change us right now.

HEAT → THORNS → CROSS → FRUIT

The Three Trees diagram appears in the study guide near the beginning of this session. There is no need to talk through the diagram again but you can say that today's session will focus on the thorns (or bad fruit) of our lives.

Dwelling on our thorns can feel quite hard. Indeed, some participants may be overwhelmed, feeling as if there is only bad in them, so at this point it is worth explaining that we are all a combination of sinner, sufferer, and saint. We all have wayward hearts. We are all impacted by the fallenness of this world. And, assuming everyone is a Christian, the Spirit of God is already at work in us, creating real beauty.

I PRODUCE THORNS

READ: COLOSSIANS 3:5–11 *(15 MINUTES)*

Have discussion partners spend a few minutes identifying the sinful responses listed in the passage and reflecting on which sinful responses are typically most tempting for them in the heat of their lives. Aim for general comments here rather than specific reflection on the homework assigned last week.

Having seen what kinds of "thorns" the Bible lists, it's time to get personal. Ask people to share with their partners the specific thorns they have seen in their own lives this week. This is the participants' chance to start talking through some of the homework from last week. You can allow about twelve minutes for this exercise.

It wouldn't be appropriate to ask people to share with the wider group. It isn't easy to share the thorns of our life, and people's struggles need to be treated with sensitivity. However, it can be useful to ask how people found the experience of sharing their thorns with another person. You might get answers like: embarrassing, exhausting, or upsetting. It can be useful to acknowledge that this kind of conversation can feel hard because we don't do it very often, but it is useful and a step toward change.

READ COLOSSIANS 3:9-17 *(10 MINUTES)*

Talk through the fact that Paul instructs us to "put off" the Gentile way of life and "put on" Christian living but, in reality, we often spend more time denying, avoiding, or blaming others for our thorny behavior. General comments can be found in the study guide but give brief, specific examples from your own life or ministry that help people understand the ungodly ways we respond to the heat in our lives.

1. Worry

2. Escapism

3. Denial

4. Anger and blame

5. Self-pity

6. Fear

7. Despair

DISCUSS *(5 MINUTES)*

Encourage people to turn to their discussion partners and give them five minutes to work through the next questions. The hope here is that people will begin to see that avoiding or denying our thorns does no one any good!

Don't spend long on feedback here, but you can pause for a moment and ask if anyone has any general observations they would like to share. Praise God if people start making comments like, "My response to heat can turn up the heat for others," or, "I have a choice. No one can force me to respond poorly." At this point you might like to throw in a note about abusive relationships. There are some marriages (or other relationships) in which one partner is extremely, maybe even violently, coercive. The other person in the relationship may have been told many times that he or she is to blame for the abuser's behavior. You can encourage people who feel they might be in that situation to talk to you privately at the end of the session or at another time. But within the session, it is time to locate the source of our thorns.

MY THORNS COME FROM MY HEART

In this section, read the passages one at a time and discuss what they show us about the source of our thorns. This can be done in one large group with you guiding the discussion.

READ: MARK 7:20–23 AND LUKE 6:43–45 *(10 MINUTES)*

1. Reflect on the fact that often we think of ourselves as basically good. If we think we're generally fine, it can be hard to understand why we behave as we do. The Bible is clear: we are not basically good; we are basically wayward (the Bible says "evil"). There is a serious problem with our hearts. When we see ourselves like this, it's not a surprise that "thorns" spring from our hearts. Some people may not like this, but keep persevering. That is what the Bible says.

READ: JAMES 4:1–3 *(15 MINUTES)*

2. James confronts us with another uncomfortable truth. We don't argue because of anything in the other person or anything the other person has done; we argue because of our heart. When we fight back, it is because we are not getting what we want and we are trying to make sure that changes. We try to push other people out of the way so our desires can be met.

3. Before leaving this tricky but important subject, it can be useful to reflect on how our heart desires grow, often with us being unaware. Here again you could use an example from your own life. Show how a preference for peace and quiet in the evening ("I like peace") can gradually grow to a desire ("I will be happy if I get peace this evening") and then a need ("I won't be able to function tomorrow if I don't get peace tonight"). After that, it can grow further still ("I work hard during the day; I deserve peace in the evening") until it becomes a demand ("Can't you leave me in peace for two minutes? Get out of my sight!"). Before we know it, something good has grown into something ugly.

This is what we are like. And so it is our hearts where change needs to begin.

DISCUSS *(10 MINUTES)*

Ask participants to meet with their discussion partners and scan down the list of diagnostic questions in the study guide. Which of these do they find most helpful in teasing out what is really going on in their heart? What *is* actually going on in their heart? You can set aside about ten minutes for this exercise.

LINK

At the end of this exercise, it can be useful to acknowledge that it can be painful to be confronted with what is going on in our hearts. Sometimes we prefer to blame others—that is more convenient. Sometimes we like our wayward hearts the way they are, because exhibiting thorns gets us what we want. Next time we are going to look at how running to the cross provides us with the forgiveness we need in order to change.

HOMEWORK

This week, participants are encouraged first to take responsibility for any sin they are identifying as part of their change project—not minimizing it or excusing it, but seeing these thorns as ours, coming from our own hearts. Secondly, and as important, it leads people not to stew in their sinfulness but to ask for forgiveness and believe that God truly does forgive them.

Encourage people to send you a 300- to 400-word summary of what they are learning about their hearts. This isn't so you can pry or grade them on their holiness. It is a useful step in helping them reflect on and be open about their struggles. If people decide to send you their summaries, respond by thanking them, perhaps asking them a question to help them progress in their thinking and praising God for the work of the Spirit so evidently active in them. And, if they have extra time, they can spend some time dwelling on the wonderful grace that God showers into the lives of those who repent (Isaiah 54:4–8; Micah 7:18–20; Luke 19:1–10).

PRAY

End the session by encouraging people to pray with their discussion partners.

SESSION 4: CROSS

AIM

To help participants reflect on the ways in which Jesus's mercies affect their past, present, and future.

DURING THE WEEK

It can be helpful to email people during the week to remind them of their homework, to let them know how to access the recordings of the first three sessions (if you've made them), and to encourage them that the process of change is going to be worthwhile. Please spend some time praying for the participants as you prepare for this fourth session.

WELCOME AND PRAYER

At the start of the session, welcome everyone back to the course and encourage them to sit with their discussion partner. As you begin, turn to the Lord in prayer. You might like to thank God for his promise to change us and thank him that one day we will be perfect.

RECAP (10 MINUTES)

Hopefully, the material is beginning to gel in people's minds, but it's useful to give a very short recap. Remind people that God is changing us in community, that he is active in every circumstance of our lives, and that we all have wayward hearts that respond wrongly to the pressures of life. You can introduce the main thrust of this session: looking at how Jesus changes everything.

While you won't discuss the details of participants' homework in front of the group (whether they emailed you their summaries or not), it can be useful to ask the group how they are finding the process of looking at their hearts. Spend a few minutes getting their feedback.

DISCUSS

Next, **reflect** on the three statements in the study guide that remind us that pursuing change can be simultaneously uncomfortable (most of us don't do things like the *Real Change* course on a regular basis); good (it's wonderful to become more like Jesus), and complex (it's best to pursue change in just one area of our lives since we can't tackle everything at once). You might like to include an example of how you, personally, relate to the statements. Then, give the participants five minutes to **discuss,** with their discussion **partners,** the ways in which they can relate to the statements. Encourage them to pray together about the things they are finding hard, encouraging, and complex.

The session now is going to turn to the cross. Here you might explain that when this course uses the word "cross," it is shorthand for everything Jesus has achieved—past, present, and future. He was born to die on the cross, he taught about what his work on the cross would achieve, he died on the cross, rose from the cross and grave, ascended after being on the cross, and now reigns in heaven. His coronation gift to his people is his Spirit. Through his Spirit he lives with his people and teaches us to respond to God as Father: loving him, loving others, and in every way growing to be more like him. He is now interceding for us, with the scars of the cross still on his body. One day he is going to return again.

CHRIST WINS OVER MY HEART

If we are to change, we all need to grow in trusting what Jesus has done for us already, what he is doing in us daily, and what he will achieve for us in the future.

READ: COLOSSIANS 3:1-4 *(10 MINUTES)*

1. We have died with Christ! The old self, the rebel alienated from God, has gone. And we have been raised with Christ! Jesus has given us a whole new life with him!

2. Our attention, therefore, needs to be "set," deliberately focused on heavenly things. There are many good things in life that are exciting and rewarding, great fun, and full of joy. But when we stop to think about it, nothing is more exciting than these "things above." When we see who Jesus is (in all his power and glory) and we see who he has made us to be (people given a new life with him by our generous God), then our new

life will obviously be the most exciting thing we ever think about. Most often, the only reason we are not more excited by it is that we are thinking about lots of other things instead of "things above." As we dwell on Jesus, we will find that sin becomes less appealing, and the thought of reflecting him becomes more appealing. We will even be willing to engage in the painful battle to the death, which Colossians 3:5 onward describes. One day, when Jesus returns, the process of change will be completed and we will be perfected, like him. There is no dream so wonderful as this—and it is true!

In your preparation for this session, be praying that participants get excited about "things above," or at least begin to want to get excited. As leader, you may need to take some prayerful time to think through what these verses mean for you personally so you can lead out of your sense of joy at what Jesus has done, and will do, for you.

DISCUSS *(5 MINUTES)*

Ask the participants to talk with their discussion partners to apply the wonderful truths of Colossians 3:1–4 to the specific issues they have been discussing in their personal change projects. After five minutes, draw everyone back together and let them know the course is now going to look at how we keep our eyes on Jesus day by day.

I LIVE BY REPENTANCE AND FAITH IN JESUS

Explain that, if change is to happen, we need to live cross-centered lives. That means living lives that are soaked through with repentance and faith. These are relational words. Repentance is before God, turning from sin and turning to God in his power, majesty, and love. Faith is personal dependence on God, on his promises in Christ. This isn't always easy, but it is precisely this relationship that is at the heart of the Christian life.

As part of last week's homework, participants should hopefully have been reflecting on Luke 15. So, after reading the passage again, you should be able to go through these questions as a whole group.

READ: LUKE 15:11–32 *(15 MINUTES)*

3. The prodigal son had big problems in his heart. He thought satisfaction lay in leaving his father so he could have a good time doing his own thing.

4. When he reached his lowest ebb—feeding the pigs, disgusted with where his choices had led him, he came to see that he was far better off at home with his father.

5. He went back to his father in utter humility. He exercised repentance (he turned around and went home) and faith (he trusted that his father would treat him with kindness and mercy).

6. Just as the father welcomed his son home with open arms, so God welcomes us in love when we return in repentance and faith.

It is worth reinforcing this final point strongly. Most well-taught Christians will know in theory that God welcomes sinners, but functionally we often live as if we need to hide from him or clean ourselves up before we repent. Encourage people to dwell on the extravagance of the father in the story: the run, the ring, the robe, the roast beef! Help them revel in the extraordinary love of their heavenly Father too.

If we are going to do the same with the many thorns in our lives, we need to know for sure what God's response will be, and why.

READ: 1 JOHN 1:9–10 AND 1 JOHN 2:1–2 *(15 MINUTES)*

7. We have an advocate in Jesus! When we stand before the judgment seat, Jesus will say, "Father, you have to forgive their sin because I died being punished for it, just as we planned." It's an argument God loves to hear and will always accept without hesitation, so we may be certain it will always work!

READ: 1 JOHN 3:1–3

8. We are now God's children and have the promise of being like him. And so we will purify ourselves because we cannot imagine a better way to be than to be more like Jesus. (This doesn't mean we will save ourselves—only Jesus can do that—but it does mean we will actively

choose to move away from sin and toward Christlikeness as we respond to his gift of salvation.)

9. As leader, please encourage (and model) appropriate excitement at these glorious truths. This grace, this adoption, this call to a new way of living is wonderful, and it's good to let people see not just the theological facts but the ways those facts motivate us to live for Christ.

The Bonar quotation in the study guide isn't the easiest, linguistically speaking, but there is real beauty in the words. It's worth reading it aloud, slowly and carefully, to let its meaning sink into our hearts.

LOOK AT YOUR OWN HEART *(10 MINUTES)*
Before the end of the session, it's important to ground our struggles in the realities of what we have been learning. Ask the participants to turn to their discussion partners again and discuss the four questions. Allow ten minutes for this and encourage them to be really specific in applying what they have been learning about repentance and faith, their new life in Christ, the gift of gospel hope, and the reason they can be confident of change.

After drawing the group back together, you might refer back to Philippians 1:6 to reinforce the point that, because of Jesus, change is happening!

HOMEWORK
Finally, talk through the homework for this week. This is an opportunity to apply the truths of the gospel to their own circumstances and to imagine how things related to their change project could become different as we all change together.

PRAY
End the session by encouraging people to pray with their discussion partners, asking for God's help to make them ever more willing to live by repentance and faith in their particular circumstances.

SESSION 5: FRUIT

AIM

To help participants reflect on the ways in which Jesus produces good fruit in their lives.

DURING THE WEEK

It can be helpful to email people during the week to remind them of their homework, to let them know how to access the recordings of the first four sessions (if you've made them) and to encourage them that the process of change is going to be worthwhile. Please also spend some time praying for the participants as you prepare for the fifth session.

WELCOME AND PRAYER

At the start of the session, welcome everyone back to the course and encourage them to sit with their discussion partners. Begin with prayer, thanking God for his promise to change us and for the wholehearted sufficiency of his promises. You might like to pray that the participants will see increasing good fruit in their lives.

RECAP *(5 MINUTES)*

Hopefully, the material is beginning to gel, but it's useful to give a very short recap. Remind people that God is changing us in community, that he is active in every circumstance of our lives, that we all have wayward hearts that respond wrongly to the pressures of life, but that the gospel changes everything. You can introduce the main thrust of this session: looking at how Jesus brings good fruit into our lives.

Before introducing today's new material, invite the participants to meet with their discussion partners to talk about how they found last week's homework. What was challenging, encouraging, confusing? What have they noticed about themselves? You can allow about five minutes for this process and then ask if a couple of people want to share their thoughts with the whole group.

FRUIT COMES FROM A CHANGED HEART

Take a few moments to read out the words of John Newton's hymn "In Evil Long I Took Delight" (words in study guide). Read slowly and thoughtfully, and encourage the participants to reflect on them as you do:

If your group would appreciate hearing it sung, "The Look" by Bob Kauflin is a beautiful arrangement: https://sovereigngracemusic.org/music/songs/the-look/. If you want to play it to them, you will need speakers and a phone or other device.[1] The "two looks" from the cross are so important. The first tells us Christ knows we are the guilty ones for whom he died. The second tells us Christ died for us out of love for us, that we are forgiven and precious to him. The first on its own is terrifying; the second on its own is incomprehensible. We must stay long enough at the cross to see both.

REFLECT *(15 MINUTES)*

Ask the participants to answer the four questions in the study guide with their discussion partners. You can allow about fifteen minutes for this. There is no need to ask for feedback on the first two questions (though you can if you have time), but it will be useful to hear more of what people are thinking in response to questions 3 and 4.

1. Encourage participants to think about how looking to Jesus on the cross changed Newton's "wild career." Hopefully the participants will, among other things, be bowled over afresh by grace.

2. Encourage people to share both the traditional and contemporary songs that are relevant to their change project.

3. The Lord, by his Spirit, nudges his children to want what he wants, so hopefully, everyone present will want to grow in a life flooded by grace and hope. But be alert to members of the group who might still be struggling and wondering if other paths might be easier. It is possible they haven't fully grasped grace; it's possible they are facing some very

---

1. In the UK, you must hold a Performing Rights License to play recorded music in a space like a church or community hall or place of work.

distracting personal situations they want to be fixed right now, or even (on rare occasions) that they haven't actually started following Jesus.

4. Reinforce once more the precious reality that change is actually happening.

LINK

Our desires, preferences, and affections have been deeply changed by the gospel. We are learning to see sin, which in the end rejects and kills Christ, as ugly instead of attractive. We are learning to see that the problem is rooted in our hearts: it's not just some random, bizarre behavior but is motivated by our disordered desires. We are doing what we really want to do! Yet, despite all this, we find that we are welcomed back by God, enabled to come back under his rule and receive his grace in forgiveness. As we freshly experience his love and grace for our sin, our desires for ourselves pale beside a growing godly ambition to be like Christ.

The Spirit of God takes the Word of God as it proclaims the Son of God crucified and raised and presses it into our hearts as the growing object of our supreme desire. "I want to know Christ—yes, to know the power of his resurrection and participation in his sufferings, becoming like him in his death, and so, somehow, attaining to the resurrection from the dead. Not that I have already obtained all this, or have already arrived at my goal, but I press on to take hold of that for which Christ Jesus took hold of me" (Philippians 3:10–12). With those words of confidence in mind, read the following verses from Titus and invite the participants to comment on what strikes them about these words.

READ: TITUS 2:11–14 *(10 MINUTES)*

Verses 13 and 14 are the driving force, not the explanatory footnote. We live every moment now as a people-in-waiting for something amazing. Our hearts *are* changed, and we are increasingly "eager to do what is good." Encourage people to meet with their discussion partner to answer the next question.

5. Encourage everyone to think about what they want to say no and yes to.

At this point, it will be useful to pause for questions. Take a few moments to make sure everyone is clear that changed behavior comes from a changed heart.

BY GRACE I CAN BEAR THE FRUIT OF CHRISTLIKENESS *(20 MINUTES)*

This is the point in the course where each aspect of the diagram is—hopefully—coming together. The next exercise encourages participants to look at a passage from Galatians and map what they find there onto the Three Trees diagram. It will be useful to provide some context from the letter. The church there was in trouble because people were teaching that you needed law as well as grace to be Christian. Paul responded by showing what real freedom is and how it should be used.

Read the passage to the whole group, then give participants about ten minutes with their discussion partners to identify the heat, thorns, cross, fruit, and aspects of reaping seen in the verses. Afterward, ask people to share their thoughts. By this stage, it's important that participants are beginning to grasp how change works.

READ: GALATIANS 5:16–6:10

6. The kinds of answers you are looking for are:

Heat: False teaching in the church / conflict within the church

Thorns/Bad fruit: Fighting / provoking / envying / factions / drunkenness / impurity (from a root of conceit)

Cross: Ask people to reword verse 24

Good fruit: Carrying one another's burdens / gentleness / self-control / restoring sinners (from a root of being in step with the Spirit)

Reaping: Encourage people to reflect on verse 8

It's worth inserting a moment of encouragement here: if change can happen in the Galatian church, it can happen in ours!

REFLECT *(10 MINUTES)*

Encourage your participants to start imagining with their discussion partners what a life with more good fruit could be like, especially in regard to the issue they have been working on in recent weeks. Ask them to read through the list of the Spirit's fruit and answer the questions. You can allow about ten minutes for this.

Help people to think confidently about a new, possible future but keep them focused on their own hearts. It is going to be far more helpful to think about a future where "I could pray and respond with love and patience when my children are disobedient" than a future where "my children will be perfectly behaved!"

FEEDBACK

There is no need to ask people to share the personal content of their conversation with their discussion partners but it is interesting to gauge how people are feeling at this point: Excited? Hopeful? Confused? Depressed? Confident? You might follow up individually with anyone who still feels as if he or she is unlikely to change. You might also set aside a few minutes for people to pray for change with their discussion partners. End by reminding people that the good news of the gospel is that this fruit grows and goes on growing. Encourage participants not to be satisfied until they have it, but at the same time grow patience while they don't!

HOMEWORK

Take a moment to review this week's homework, which comes in two parts. First, participants will look at how a passage of Scripture has changed them in the past. This is to help them reflect on the reality that God has been at work in them by his Word. When they are thinking about a part of the Bible that has been deeply meaningful, almost always they will be thinking about how it has changed them in some way. Second, they will look at how to apply what they have been learning this week to the issues they are seeking to change.

The course is almost at an end now. It is worth letting people know that at the end of the next session, they will be offered the chance to complete two things:

>> A short questionnaire to be filled out on the final night

>> A page of 350 to 400 words tracking themselves around the Three Trees diagram and the progress they made in understanding how the gospel brings change and any changes they might have seen in themselves. There is no pressure to do this. If they do it, there is no pressure to show masses of change. It is better to be real about where they really are.)

PRAY
End the session by praying for the group, being thankful for the cross and full of hope for the future.

SESSION 6: REAL CHANGE

AIM

To help participants persevere in a lifelong journey of change with their eyes firmly fixed on Jesus.

DURING THE WEEK

It can be helpful to email people during the week to remind them of their homework, to let them know how to access the recordings of the first five sessions (if you've made them) and to encourage them that the process of change is going to be worthwhile. Please spend some time praying for the participants as you prepare for this final session.

WELCOME AND PRAYER

Welcome everyone back to the course and encourage them to sit with their discussion partners. As you begin, turn to the Lord in prayer, thanking him for the ways the participants have already been changing. Ask him to help everyone keep their eyes fixed on Jesus.

RECAP *(5 MINUTES)*

Hopefully, the diagram feels familiar at this point, but it's worth running through it one more time. Some participants might notice that each time the recap section appears in the handbook, the words change a little. That's to encourage us to remember that there are different ways of expressing these exciting truths.

As you begin, remind the group of some of the wonderful truths of Philippians 1 that we considered in the first session. You might read out verse 6 and remind people that God is going to continue working in their lives until all the work is done. You might read out verse 27 and reflect that everything in our lives, big and small, needs to be shaped by the gospel.

DISCUSS *(10 MINUTES)*

Before introducing tonight's new material, leave an opportunity for questions and comments. If anyone is still confused about any aspect of the diagram, now is the time for them to ask questions. Next, encourage people to meet with their discussion partner and talk about their struggles and hopes, using the diagram as a template. (Ask them to briefly describe their heat, thorns, heart, etc.).

Some people find it hard to imagine what change looks like. Some assume that we simply have to understand ourselves better; some assume the process should be fast (if not instant); some assume they will be able to conquer their sins this side of heaven, and some may still feel as if they won't really make much progress. The next section is designed to help people to be realistic about what lies ahead.

WHAT DOES REAL CHANGE LOOK LIKE?

CLARIFY FOUR THINGS ABOUT REAL CHANGE *(5 MINUTES)*

Using examples from your own life, explain that we should expect to see tangible differences in our lives as God works in us but that this takes time, and won't be complete this side of heaven. End on a note of confidence that change is happening. Sample Bible verses can be found in the study guide but you might like to include other material as well. A good place to end could be 2 Corinthians 3:18.

DISCUSS *(3-5 MINUTES)*

Ask the participants to talk with their discussion partners about which of the four statements listed they need to remember most. Allow about three minutes for this and then ask for some brief feedback.

HOW DO WE KEEP GOING?

Encourage participants to make sure they keep on living in ways that promote change. Remind them of the different types of input and encouragement that the *Real Change* course has provided (Bible teaching, prayer, the Three Trees model, discussion, accountability, structure, and written tasks).

DISCUSS (7–10 MINUTES)

Ask the participants to reflect with their discussion partners on what insights and practical points from this course have been useful. Encourage them to think about *why* these things have been helpful. The seven things listed in the study guide are key examples of the things they might choose but there may have been other helpful aspects too. Note: This is not the time to focus on how they have changed through their personal change project but to reflect on what overarching things they have learned that can be carried over into other situations. You can allow about seven minutes for this and then ask people to give feedback. Hopefully it will be a huge encouragement to hear what people have found useful!

Next, ask them to think through, with their discussion partners, how they can keep engaging with God's Word, prayer, people, reflection, etc. in the coming weeks. If the discussion pairs are working well, you might suggest that they keep meeting together regularly or occasionally. Allow about six minutes for this. Feel free to invite brief feedback if there is time.

LINK

Spend some time reflecting on the fact that this course isn't meant to be a special thing that happens occasionally. This kind of thinking and praying is meant to be a normal part of church life. Obviously, church is more than a place of change, but it should never be less than a place of change. This next section is designed to show how we can take every opportunity to apply what we are learning at church to our own hearts.

THIS IS REAL CHURCH! *(10 MINUTES)*

Ask the participants to think back, with their discussion partners, to the last sermon they heard, the last Bible study they attended (group or one-on-one) or the last quiet time they had. Ask them to think about what the Scriptures they looked at had to say about the struggles they have been focusing on during this course. Obviously, not everyone will be able to comment on all four areas listed (and we don't want to induce guilt about that), but hopefully everyone can do at least one. Allow about ten minutes for this.

We can't expect every sermon and Bible study to speak directly to the specific concerns that are highest in our minds at any given time—the Bible does not serve our agenda—but we should expect God to address us through his Word.

LINK

Spend a few moments talking through the ways these four types of engagement with God's Word can help us change. Sermons are community activities where we sit quietly and humbly before the Word. Bible studies and one-on-ones are opportunities for deeper reflection and more open sharing. Personal quiet times are great opportunities for heartfelt prayer and confession. Highlight some of the questions in the study guide. These are great things for participants to be asking themselves on a regular basis. Doing so is part of what it means to continue growing.

DISCUSS *(5 MINUTES)*

Ask the participants, with their discussion partners, to think about what attitudes they can have toward each of these four activities. In the future, will they participate in these activities any differently? Allow about five minutes for this. Afterward, you can ask for feedback. Hopefully you will get some comments like:

- » I'm going to try to talk about the sermon, and how it connected with me, with someone after church.

- » I'm going to share a prayer request that revolves around my heart rather than my actions.

- » I'm going to keep a journal of what I am learning in Bible study and how it applies to my desires.

- » I am going to start reading the Bible with someone and make myself accountable for some of the things I'm struggling with.

Encourage the group to make the most of every opportunity to seek growth.

REFLECT *(10 MINUTES)*

As the course comes to an end, encourage the participants to turn to their discussion partners and celebrate how they think they have grown through their personal change project, along with any other points of thanksgiving. How can they see real change in their hearts and in their lives? Allow a good ten minutes to share encouragements and pray together.

Ask participants to complete the feedback form and encourage them to complete the final piece of homework, which is summarizing their personal change project in writing by showing how they have worked through each element of the Three Trees diagram. This homework isn't an opportunity for the leader to pry into what is happening in people's lives, but a good way of encouraging participants to reflect on their progress. It's not compulsory for people to do this homework, so don't force the issue. But it's good to encourage them to try. Once you have received each response, take a moment to pray for the person and respond to their email with a suitably encouraging, Jesus-centered response. If you pick up on any serious pastoral situations, invite the people involved to meet with you or another suitable person within the church as soon as possible.

Close the evening with an encouragement to keep going and a prayer.

Christian Counseling & Educational Foundation

CCEF's mission is to restore Christ to
counseling and counseling to the church
by thinking biblically about the issues
of living in order to equip the church to
meet counseling-related needs.

For other resources like these,
please visit **ccef.org**